Hitler and the Sec

A collection of writings by

Julius Evola

Articles Originally published in Italian and German language.
English-language edition copyright © 2019 by *Artemis Press*.

"WE ARE BORN INTO THIS TIME AND MUST BRAVELY FOLLOW THE PATH TO THE DESTINED END. THERE IS NO OTHER WAY. OUR DUTY IS TO HOLD ON TO THE LOST POSITION, WITHOUT HOPE, WITHOUT RESCUE, LIKE THAT ROMAN SOLDIER WHOSE BONES WERE FOUND IN FRONT OF A DOOR IN POMPEII, WHO DIED AT HIS POST DURING THE ERUPTION OF VESUVIUS BECAUSE SOMEONE FORGOT TO RELIEVE HIM. THAT IS GREATNESS. THAT IS WHAT IT MEANS TO BE A THOROUGHBRED. THE HONORABLE END IS THE ONE THAT CAN NOT BE TAKEN FROM A MAN."

— OSWALD SPENGLER

"MY ASSERTION THAT TODAY THERE IS NO POLITICAL SYSTEM, NO FORMATION, AND NO PARTY WHATSOEVER WORTH DEVOTING ONESELF TO, AND THAT EVERYTHING EXISTING MUST BE DENIED, HAS DISCONCERTED MANY. HOWEVER, THIS DENIAL AND NON-COMMITMENT DO NOT DERIVE FROM A LACK OF PRINCIPLES, BUT FROM THE POSSESSION OF PRINCIPLES, WHICH ARE PRECISE, SOLID AND NOT SUBJECT TO COMPROMISE."

— JULIUS EVOLA

writings presented in this book:

- "Hitler and the Secret Societies", from "Il Conciliatore", no. 10, 1971; translated from the German edition in Deutsche Stimme, no. 8, 1998.
- "On the Secret of Degeneration", from Deutsches Volkstum, Nr. 11, 1938.
- "American 'Civilization'"; from "Civiltà Americana", Fondazione. Julius Evola 1983, appeard on «Corriere Padano», «Il Nazionale» and «Meridiano d'Italia», between 1942 and 1955.
- "Against the Neo-Pagans"; Extract from "Grundrisse" (1942).
- "The Meaning and Context of Zen"; from "Lo Zen", Roma, Fondazione Julius Evola, Quaderni di testi evoliani, n° 15, 1981. Tra. by Guido Stucco.
- "Yoga, Immortality and Freedom"; from "East and West", vol. 6, no. 3 (1955): 224–30.
- "Fascism: Myth and Reality"; from "Il fascisimo", Rome, 1979; 1st edn. 1964.
- "The Nature of Initiatic Knowledge"; Excerpt from "Gli Uomini e le Rovine", Ed. Dell'Ascia, 1953.
- "Synthesis of a Doctrine of Race"; Excerpt from parts two and three of *Synthesis of a Doctrine of Race* (1941), (an Article written at Mussolini's request).
- "The Occult War"; Excerpt from "Gli Uomini e le Rovine", Ed. dell'Ascia, 1953.

Table of Contents

On the Author: Julius Evola	vii
Hitler and the Secret Societies	Pg. 1
On the Secret of Degeneration	Pg. 8
American "Civilization"	Pg. 15
Against the Neo-Pagans	Pg. 24
The Meaning and Context of Zen	Pg. 33
Yoga, Immortality and Freedom	Pg. 42
Fascism: Myth and Reality	Pg. 57
The Nature of Initiatic Knowledge	Pg. 59
Synthesis of a Doctrine of Race	Pg. 68
The Occult War	Pg. 74

According to Plato a primordial race existed "whose essence is now extinct," a race of beings who contained in themselves both principles, male and female. This hermaphroditic race "was extraordinarily strong and brave, and they nourished in their hearts very arrogant designs, even unto an attack upon the god themselves...."

According to Plato the gods did not strike the hermaphrodites with lightening...but paralyzed their power and broke them in two. Thenceforth there arouse beings of one sex or the other, male or female; they were, however, beings who retained the memory of their earlier state and in whom the impulse to reconstitute the primordial unity was kindled. According to Plato, in that impulse should be sought the ultimate metaphysical and everlasting meaning of eros: "From such an ancient time has love goaded human beings one toward the other; it is inborn and seeks to renew our ancient nature in an endeavor to unite in one single being two distinct beings...."

"It is really the burning longing for this unity which bears the name of love."

– Julius Evola (The Metaphysics of Sex)

JULIUS EVOLA

Julius Evola, also known as Baron Giulio Cesare Andrea Evola (19 May 1898 - 11 June 1974) was an Italian philosopher and esoteric scholar, author, artist, poet, political activist, and soldier. Evola was raised a strict Catholic. Despite this, his life was characterized by 'an anti-bourgeois approach' hostile to both 'the dominant tradition of the West – Christianity and Catholicism – and to contemporary civilization – the 'modern world' of democracy and materialism'. Author of many books on esoteric, political and religious topics (including The Hermetic Tradition, The Doctrine of Awakening and Eros and the Mysteries of Love), his best-known work remains Revolt Against the Modern World, a trenchant critique of modern civilization that has been described as 'the gateway to his thought'.

Since his death, his writings have influenced right-wing, reactionary and conservative political thought not only in his native Italy, but throughout continental Europe and, increasingly, the English-speaking world. Nevertheless, he should not be considered primarily as a political thinker, but rather as an exponent of the wider Traditionalist School that encompasses the work of such individuals as René Guénon, Titus Burckhardt and Frithjof Schuon.

Evola's earliest years remain obscure - so obscure as to move one commentator to observe it was if he "seems never to have been a child, but to have come into the world fully-formed, ready for his life's mission at a time when most young men are still finding themselves."

According to *The Path of Cinnabar*, besides the study of technical and mathematical subjects, Evola's teenage years brought a spontaneous interest in thought and art, one which led him to writers like Oscar Wilde and Gabriele D'Annunzio, which only deepened his engagement with contemporary art and literature. There were other influences, of a more philosophical nature. These included Otto Weininger, Carlo Michelstaedter and, especially, Friedrich Nietzsche, whose writings Evola credited with affirming him in his own 'indifference' to Christianity and revulsion towards petty moralism and conformism.

By the eve of World War I, he had begun to move in artistic circles, particularly those of the avant-garde movement of Futurism, of whose founder, F.T. Marinetti, he claimed to be an acquaintance. However, although it appears Evola had indeed become interested in painting by this time, he also felt Futurism's overall character did not appeal, other than in its revolutionary character. With war looming, Evola trained as an artillery officer and was assigned to a combat line near Asiago. However, as his unit "never engaged in any significant military operations", his experience of war and military life remained limited, as he himself acknowledged.

Following World War I Evola's attention turn to the spiritual, the occult and the philosophical, initially through various occultist, anthroposophist, and theosophist writings. In time, he came to feel these served mostly 'to discredit rather than valorise traditional doctrines'; nonetheless, it was in this milieu that he encountered Lao Tzu's *Tao Te Ching*, which appears to have acted as a point of departure for his 'philosophical phase'.

From 1921 to 1927, in Essays on Magical Idealism, The Theory and Phenomenology of the Absolute Individual, and The Individual and the Becoming of the World, Evola sought to delineate a system of philosophy that not only offered a critique of abstract Idealism, but also posited the "Absolute Individual", and the possibility of experiencing "pure being...anterior to any content determined by consciousness and thought". Though received with interest by non-specialists, his contributions to the field of speculative philosophy remained largely ignored in academe. This lack of reaction appears not to have surprised Evola (at least in retrospect), and even he admitted that his was a "philosophical introduction to a non-philosophical world" - one directed perhaps as much at himself as anyone else. Thus, by 1927, he had for the most part left the domain of 'discursive thought and speculation' behind and entered that of 'inner, self-fulfilling action'.

From at least 1924, Evola had contributed articles and essays to a variety of theosophical and philosophical journals, amongst them Atanor and Ignis, both edited by Arturo Reghini. Reghini was a Florentine traditionalist and exponent of "an unmitigated, intransigent, anti-Christian, pagan directive", who emphasized the sacred character of many aspects of pagan Roman civilization Given that Pagan Imperialism dates to this time, his influence on Evola is clear; indeed, Evola credits him with having first introduced him to the writings of René Guénon.

It appears it was also Reghini who encouraged Evola to form and lead the UR Group (Gruppo di Ur) in 1927. Based in Rome (with dependent offshoots in other cities), it sought to practically explore "esoteric and initiatory disciplines in a serious and rigorous manner by means of a critical engagement with genuine primary sources." A monthly journal, UR, dealt with specific topics, and these later were collected and published as Introduction to Magic. According to Evola, its "most ambitious goal" was to evoke a "power from on high", one that could have been directed to realize practically the ambitions and ideals set forth in Pagan Imperialism.

This was not to be. By October 1928, tensions within the group had risen such that Reghini and other inner circle members attempted to remove Evola. They failed, yet this action effectively marked the group's end, certainly in an operative sense. In December 1929, the final issue of the now-titled Krur announced what Renato del Ponte has characterized as a shift "from esotericism to traditional action": "what had been acquired on the esoteric plane of operative magic came to be integrated...into an existential-political picture".

The early thirties saw the publication of The Hermetic Tradition, a study of alchemical hermeticism from an initiatory perspective, and The Mask and Face of Contemporary Spiritualism, a traditionalist critique of, amongst other topics, Psychoanalysis, Theosophy, Anthroposophy, and

Spiritualism. Both give witness to Evola's essentially aristocratic approach to matters of the spirit, in particular the second, which condemns neospiritualism's tendency to not only popularize esoteric doctrine, but to turn the resulting pabulum into a commodity for the masses. However, although The Mask and Face of Contemporary Spiritualism was intended to elucidate "the true nature of the views" advocated by Evola, in truth it was his next work, *Revolt Against the Modern World*, that most fully achieved this. First published in 1934, it is at once "a study of the morphology of civilization and history" and "a denunciation of the regressive character of the modern world and of modern civilization". Divided into two sections, the first draws upon a range of ancient sources – both Eastern and Western – to define and outline the traditional understanding of such issues as jurisprudence and law; ritual, war and victory; property, space and time; art and games. The second section offers an interrogation of the modern world from this same traditionalist perspective.

For the author, the ideas "expressed in *Revolt* provided the foundation and yardstick for any kind of action: by shunning all compromises, illusions and pretenses, the book pointed to those values never to be forgotten." Indeed, it is precisely due his to "shunning all compromises" on those ideas that Evola's relations with the Fascist and National Socialist governments were often tense – and occasionally hostile. Regardless, *Revolt Against the Modern World* remains perhaps his greatest legacy and, in Joscelyn Godwin's words, "the gateway to his thought". Despite later efforts to categorize Evola as a Fascist or National Socialist thinker, in reality 'Official Fascism did not think highly of him', while SS reports betray a distinct antipathy towards him. This is hardly surprising, considering the highly critical stance he adopted on a range of issues relevant to both the Fascist and National Socialist ideologies, not least that of race. Benito Mussolini's ascent to power was, to Evola's unapologetically aristocratic and monarchist perspective, inappropriate. Despite his sympathies for any who might stand against leftist and democratist forces, the Fascist revolution was, in a sense, a counterfeit one. It lacked any connection to a transcendent source of power. And though its early republican, 'secular' character was soon ameliorated through fusion with Italian bourgeois "nationalist infatuations", this also blunted whatever revolutionary potential it possessed.

For Evola the 'true revolution' – the one that ought to have taken place – was one "from above", led by the sovereign himself. Still, it must be admitted that despite severe reservations, he did consider Mussolini's government as better than the alternative of liberal democracy or communism. His attitude to Fascism has been described as following the sequence of "first a great hope", then "the hope of making corrections of a traditional kind", then "a recognition that everything is lost", leading ultimately to apoliteia.

Disillusionment with Fascism led Evola to see Germany's National Socialism as "much more consequential". However, even in this case, the absence of any transcendent background to NS was to lead to the criticism of core elements of NS ideology: the great attachment to nature, a Fuhrer principle that lacked any legitimization other than that of the people and, not insignificantly, its purely biological racism. As with Fascism, Evola's ideas were just too different from official National Socialist thought. This difference is perhaps most stark in the area of race. Although Evola recognized that race was important, it was "hierarchically below the all-important primal ideas". The biological element was never enough for him: "In a cat or a thoroughbred horse the biological is the deciding element, and thus the racial observation can be restricted to this criterion. This, however, is no longer the case when dealing with humans, or at least with beings that are worthy of that name. Man is indeed a biological being, but also connected to forces and laws of a different kind, that are as real and effective as the biological realm and whose influence on the latter cannot be overlooked." This nuanced stance also conditioned his approach to questions surrounding Jewish identity, character and influence.

Before and during World War II, Evola concentrated intensely on Buddhism, which he described as a path to spiritual freedom that maintained its validity even in modern times. Evola almost exclusively referred to the Pali canon, and he pointed out that the historical Buddha was a member of the warrior caste. Evola rejected the widespread teaching of modern Mahāyāna Buddhism, which sets peacefulness and universal love in the foreground, instead of clear initiatory knowledge through asceticism and exercise. Nevertheless, Anagarika Govinda (1898–1985), who was the first Westerner to receive the title of lama, praised Evola's work.

In 1940 Evola wrote an article for the magazine *Asiatica*, published by Tucci. This work was later continued in the subsequent renowned journal *East and West*, which Tucci also managed. Another well-known Orientalist with whom Evola had been closely connected since his youth was Pio Filippani-Ronconi who taught at the University of Naples. A close friendship on the basis of common esoteric interests connected Evola with the Egyptologist Boris de Rachewiltz (1926–1997). He was also well acquainted with the historian and researcher of ancient Roman religion, Franz Altheim (1898–1976).

Whilst researching the archives secret societies on behalf of the Ahnenerbe, an appendage of the Schutzstaffel (SS), shortly before the Red Army took Vienna, Evola was seriously wounded in an airstrike, which was to leave him paralyzed from the waist down for the remainder of his life.

He returned to Italy in 1946 – first to Varese, then Bologna, before finally returning to Rome in 1948. By 1949 he was contributing to new rightist publications and soon gathered a circle of mostly young activists and radicals, though his influence on the neofascist scene was limited; his antimodernism being simply too radical. Despite this, in 1951 he was arrested and charged with "glorification of fascism" and of being an "intellectual instigator" of secret combat groups. He was acquitted. During this period, works included *Men Among the Ruins*, *Riding the Tiger*, and *The Metaphysics of Sex*, as well as a spiritual autobiography, *The Path of Cinnabar*. His final years were marked by severe pain, and he reportedly became quite embittered. He died in Rome, on 11 June 1974. His body was cremated in Spoleto and, in accordance with his wishes, the urn with his ashes was placed in a glacial crevasse on Monte Rosa.

Hitler and the Secret Societies

It is remarkable that some authors in France have researched the relationship of German National Socialism to secret societies and initiatic organizations. The motivation for this was the supposed occult background of the Hitler movement. This thesis was first proposed in the well-known and very far-fetched book by Pauwels and Bergier, "Le Matin des Magiciens" (English ed., "The Dawn of Magic"), in which National Socialism was defined as the union of "magical thinking" with technology. The expression used for this was "Tank divisions plus René Guénon": a phrase that might well have caused that eminent representative of traditional thought and esoteric disciplines to turn indignantly in his grave. The first misunderstanding here is the confusion of the magical element with the mythical, whereas the two have nothing to do with one another. The role of myths in National Socialism is undeniable, for example in the idea of the Reich, the charismatic Führer, Race, Blood, etc. But rather than calling these "myths," one should apply to them Sorel's concept of "motivating energy-ideas" (which is what all the suggestive ideas used by demagogues commonly are), and not attribute to them any magical ingredient. Similarly, no rational person thinks of magic in connection with the myths of Fascism, such as the myth of Rome or that of the Duce, any more than with those of the French Revolution or Communism. The investigation would proceed differently if one went on the assumption that certain movements, without knowing it, were subject to influences that were not merely human. But this is not the case with the French authors. They are not thinking of influences of that kind, but of a concrete nature, exercised by organizations that really existed, among which were some that to various degrees were "secret." Likewise, some have spoken of "unknown superiors" who are supposed to have called forth the National Socialist movement and to have used Hitler as a medium, though it is unclear what goals they could have had in mind in so doing. If one considers the results, the catastrophic consequences to which National Socialism led, even indirectly, those goals must have been obscure and destructive. One would have to identify the "occult side" of this movement with what Guénon called the "Counter-Initiation." But the French authors have also proposed the thesis that Hitler the "medium" emancipated himself at a certain point from the "unknown superiors," almost like a Golem, and that the movement then pursued its fatal direction. But in that case one must admit that these "unknown superiors" can have had no prescience and very limited power, to have been incapable of putting a stop to their supposed medium, Hitler.

A lot of fantasy has been woven on the concrete level about the origin of National Socialism's themes and symbols. Reference has been made to certain organizations as forerunners, but ones to which it is very difficult to attribute any genuine and factual initiatic character. There is no doubt that Hitler did not invent German racial doctrine, the symbol of the swastika, or Aryan antisemitism; all of these had long existed in Germany. A book entitled "Der Mann, der Hitler die Ideen gab" [The man who gave Hitler his ideas] reports on Jörg Lanz von Liebenfels (the title of nobility was self-bestowed), who had formerly been a Cistercian monk and had founded an Order that already used the swastika; Lanz edited the periodical "Ostara" from 1905 onwards, which Hitler certainly knew, in which the Aryan and antisemitic racial theories were already clearly worked out. But much more important for the "occult background" of National Socialism is the role of the Thule Society. Things are more complex here. This society grew out of the Germanenorden, founded in 1912, and was led by Rudolf von Sebottendorf, who had been in the East and had published a strange booklet on "Die Praxis der alten türkischen Freimaurerei" [The practice of ancient Turkish Freemasonry]. Practices were described therein that involved the repetition of syllables, gestures, and steps, whose goal was the initiatic transformation of man, such as alchemy had also aimed at. It is unclear what Turkish masonic organization Sebottendorf was in contact with, and also whether he himself practiced the things in question, or merely described them. Moreover, it cannot be established whether these practices were employed in the Thule Society that Sebottendorf headed. It would be very important to know that, because many top-ranking National Socialist personalities, from Hitler to Rudolf Hess, frequented this society. In a way, Hitler was already introduced to the world of ideas of the Thule Society by Hess during their imprisonment together after the failed Munich Putsch.

At all events, it must be emphasized that the Thule Society was less an initiatic organization than it was a secret society, which already bore the swastika and was marked by a decided antisemitism and by Germanic racial thinking. One should be cautious about the thesis that the name Thule is a serious and conscious reference to a Nordic, Polar connection, in the effort to make a connection with the Hyperborean origins of the Indo-Germans--since Thule appears in ancient tradition as the sacred center or sacred island in the uttermost North. Thule may just be a play on the name "Thale," a location in the Harz where the Germanenorden held a conference in 1914, at which it was decided to create a secret "völkisch" band to combat the supposed Jewish International. Above all, these ideas were emphasized by Sebottendorf in his book "Bevor Hitler kam" [Before Hitler came], published in Munich in 1933, in which he indicated the myths and the "völkisch" world-view that existed before Hitler. Thus a serious investigation into Hitler's initiatic connections with secret societies does not lead far.

A few explanations are necessary in regard to Hitler as a "medium" and his attractive power. It seems to us pure fantasy that he owed this power to initiatic practices. Otherwise one would have to assume the same about the psychic power of other leaders, like Mussolini and Napoleon, which is absurd. It is much better to go on the assumption that there is a psychic vortex that arises from mass movements, and that this concentrates on the man in the center and lends him a certain radiation that is felt especially by suggestible people. The quality of medium (which, to put it bluntly, is the antithesis of an initiatic qualification) can be attributed to Hitler with a few reservations, because in a certain respect he did appear as one possessed (which differentiates him from Mussolini, for example). When he whipped up the masses to fanaticism, one had the impression that another force was directing him as a medium, even though he was a man of a very extraordinary kind, and extremely gifted. Anyone who has heard Hitler's addresses to the enraptured masses can have no other impression.

Since we have already expressed our reservations about the assumption that "unknown superiors" were involved, it is not easy to define the nature of this supra-personal force.

In respect to National Socialist theosophy [Gotteserkenntnis], i.e. to its supposed mystical and metaphysical dimension, one must realize the unique juxtaposition in this movement and in the Third Reich of mythical, Enlightenment, and even scientific aspects. In Hitler, one can find many symptoms of a typically "modern" world-view that was fundamentally profane, naturalistic, and materialistic; while on the other hand he believed in Providence, whose tool he believed himself to be, especially in regard to the destiny of the German nation. (For example, he saw a sign of Providence in his survival of the assassination attempt in his East-Prussian headquarters.)

Alfred Rosenberg, the ideologist of the movement, proclaimed the myth of Blood, in which he spoke of the "mystery" of Nordic blood and attributed to it a sacramental value; yet he simultaneously attacked all the rites and sacraments of Catholicism as delusions, just like a man of the Enlightenment. He railed against the "Dark men of our time," while attributing to Aryan man the merit of having created modern science. National Socialism's concern with runes, the ancient Nordic-Germanic letter-signs, must be regarded as purely symbolic, rather like the Fascist use of certain Roman symbols, and without any esoteric significance. The program of National Socialism to create a higher man has something of "biological mysticism" about it, but this again was a scientific project. At best, it might have been a question of the "superman" in Nietzsche's sense, but never of a higher man in the initiatic sense.

The plan to "create a new racial, religious, and military Order of initiates, assembled around a divinized Führer," cannot be regarded as the official policy of National Socialism, as René Alleau writes, when he presents such a relationship and even compares it, among others, to the Ishmaelites of Islam. A few elements of a higher level were visible only in the ranks of the SS. In the first place, one can see clearly the intention of Reichsführer-SS Heinrich Himmler to create an Order in which elements of Prussian ethics were to be combined with those of the old Orders of knighthood, especially the Teutonic Order. He was looking for legitimation of such an organization, but could not obtain it, since these old Orders of Catholicism were openly opposed by the radical wing of National Socialism. Himmler was also seeking, without the possibility of any traditional connection, a relationship to the Nordic-Hyperborean heritage and its symbolism (Thule), albeit without those "secret societies" discussed above having any influence over it. He took notice, as did Rosenberg, of the researches of the Netherlander Herman Wirth into the Nordic-Atlantic tradition. Later Himmler founded, with Wirth, the research and teaching organization called the "Ahnenerbe." This is not without interest, but there was no "occult background" to it.

So the net result is negative. The French authors' fantasy reaches its high point in the book "Hitler et la tradition cathare" by Jean-Michel Angebert (Paris, 1971). This deals with the Cathars, also called Albigensians, who were a heretical sect that spread especially in Southern France between the 11th and 12th centuries, and had their center in the fortress of Montségur. According to Otto Rahn, this was destroyed in a "crusade against the Grail," which is the title of one of his books. Whatever the Grail and its Grail-Knights had to do with this sect remains completely in the dark. The sect was marked by a kind of fanatical Manicheism; sometimes its own believers would die of hunger or some other cause as a demonstration of their detachment from the world and their hostility to earthly existence in flesh and matter. Now it is assumed that Rahn, with whom we corresponded during his lifetime and tried to persuade of the baselessness of his thesis, was an SS man, and that an expedition was sent on its way to retrieve the legendary Grail which was supposedly brought to safety at the moment when the Cathars' fortress in Montségur was destroyed. After the fall of Berlin, a unit is said to have reached the Zillertal and hidden this object at the foot of a glacier, to await a new age. The truth is that there was talk of a commando unit, which however had a less mystical commission, namely the rescue and concealment of the Reich's treasures. Two further examples show what such fantasies can lead to when they are given free rein. The SS (which included not only battle units but also researchers and scholarly experts) mounted an expedition to Tibet in order to make discoveries in the fields of alpinism and ethnology, and another one to the Arctic, ostensibly for scientific research but also with a view to the possible situation of a German military base. According to these fantastic interpretations, the first expedition was seeking a link to a secret center of the Tradition, while the other was seeking contact with the lost Hyperborean Thule...

On the Secret of Degeneration

Anyone who has come to reject the rationalist myth of "progress" and the interpretation of history as an unbroken positive development of mankind will find himself gradually drawn towards the world-view that was common to all the great traditional cultures, and which had at its center the memory of a process of degeneration, slow obscuration, or collapse of a higher preceding world. As we penetrate deeper into this new (and old) interpretation, we encounter various problems, foremost among which is the question of the secret of degeneration. In its literal sense, this question is by no means a novel one. While contemplating the magnificent remains of cultures whose very name has not even come down to us, but which seem to have conveyed, even in their physical material, a greatness and power that is more than earthly, scarcely anyone has failed to ask themselves questions about the death of cultures, and sensed the inadequacy of the reasons that are usually given to explain it. We can thank the Comte de Gobineau for the best and best-known summary of this problem, and also for a masterly criticism of the main hypotheses about it. His solution on the basis of racial thought and racial purity also has a lot of truth in it, but it needs to be expanded by a few observations concerning a higher order of things. For there have been many cases in which a culture has collapsed even when its race has remained pure, as is especially clear in certain groups that have suffered slow, inexorable extinction despite remaining as racially isolated as if they were islands. An example quite close at hand is the case of the Swedes and the Dutch. These people are in the same racial condition today as they were two centuries ago, but there is little to be found now of the heroic disposition and the racial awareness that they once possessed. Other great cultures seem merely to have remained standing in the condition of mummies: they have long been inwardly dead, so that it takes only the slightest push to knock them down. This was the case, for example, with ancient Peru, that giant solar empire which was annihilated by a few adventurers drawn from the worst rabble of Europe.

If we look at the secret of degeneration from the exclusively traditional point of view, it becomes even harder to solve it completely. It is then a matter of the division of all cultures into two main types. On the one hand there are the traditional cultures, whose principle is identical and unchangeable, despite all the differences evident on the surface. The axis of these cultures and the summit of their hierarchical order consists of metaphysical, supra-individual powers and actions, which serve to inform and justify everything that is merely human, temporal, subject to becoming and to "history." On the other hand there is "modern culture," which is actually the anti-tradition and which exhausts itself in a construction of purely human and earthly conditions and in the total development of these, in pursuit of a life entirely detached from the "higher world." From the standpoint of the latter, the whole of history is degeneration, because it shows the universal decline of earlier cultures of the traditional type, and the decisive and violent rise of a new universal civilization of the "modern" type. A double question arises from this.

First, how was it ever possible for this to come to pass? There is a logical error underlying the whole doctrine of evolution: it is impossible that the higher can emerge from the lower, and the greater from the less. But doesn't a similar difficulty face us in the solution of the doctrine of involution? How is it ever possible for the higher to fall? If we could make do with simple analogies, it would be easy to deal with this question. A healthy man can become sick; a virtuous one can turn to vice. There is a natural law that everyone takes from granted: that every living being starts with birth, growth, and strength, then come old age, weakening, and disintegration. And so forth. But this is just making statements, not explaining, even if we allow that such analogies actually relate to the question posed here. Secondly, it is not only a matter of explaining the possibility of the degeneration of a particular cultural world, but also the possibility that the degeneration of one cultural cycle may pass to other peoples and take them down with it. For example, we have not only to explain how the ancient Western reality collapsed, but also have to show the reason why it was possible for "modern" culture to conquer practically the whole world, and why it possessed the power to divert so many peoples from any other type of culture, and to hold sway even where states of a traditional kind seemed to be alive (one need only recall the Aryan East). In this respect, it is not enough to say that we are dealing with a purely material and economic conquest. That view seems very superficial, for two reasons. In the first place, a land that is conquered on the material level also experiences, in the long run, influences of a higher kind corresponding to the cultural type of its conqueror. We can state, in fact, that European conquest almost everywhere sows the seeds of "Europeanization," i.e., the "modern" rationalist, tradition-hostile, individualistic way of thinking.

Secondly, the traditional conception of culture and the state is hierarchical, not dualistic. Its bearers could never subscribe, without severe reservations, to the principles of "Render unto Caesar the things that are Caesar's" and "My kingdom is not of this world." For us, "Tradition" is the victorious and creative presence in the world of that which is "not of this world," i.e., of the Spirit, understood as a power that is mightier than any merely human or material one.

This is a basic idea of the authentically traditional view of life, which does not permit us to speak with contempt of merely material conquests. On the contrary, the material conquest is the sign, if not of a spiritual victory, at least of a spiritual weakness or a kind of spiritual "retreat" in the cultures that are conquered and lose their independence. Everywhere that the Spirit, regarded as the stronger power, was truly present, it never lacked for means – visible or otherwise – to enable all the opponent's technical and material superiority to be resisted. But this has not happened. It must be concluded, then, that degeneracy was lurking behind the traditional facade of every people that the "modern" world has been able to conquer. The West must then have been the culture in which a crisis that was already universal assumed its acutest form. There the degeneration amounted, so to speak, to a knockout blow, and as it took effect, it brought down with more or less ease other peoples in whom the involution had certainly not "progressed" as far, but whose tradition had already lost its original power, so that these peoples were no longer able to protect themselves from an outside assault.

With these considerations, the second aspect of our problem is traced back to the first one. It is mainly a question of explicating the meaning and the possibility of degeneracy, without reference to other circumstances. For this we must be clear about one thing: it is an error to assume that the hierarchy of the traditional world is based on a tyranny of the upper classes. That is merely a "modern" conception, completely alien to the traditional way of thinking. The traditional doctrine in fact conceived of spiritual action as an "action without acting"; it spoke of the "unmoved mover"; everywhere it used the symbolism of the "pole," the unalterable axis around which every ordered movement takes place (and elsewhere we have shown that this is the meaning of the swastika, the "arctic cross"); it always stressed the "Olympian," spirituality, and genuine authority, as well as its way of acting directly on its subordinates, not through violence but through "presence"; finally, it used the simile of the magnet, wherein lies the key to our question, as we shall now see.

Only today could anyone imagine that the authentic bearers of the Spirit, or of Tradition, pursue people so as to seize them and put them in their places – in short, that they "manage" people, or have any personal interest in setting up and maintaining those hierarchical relationships by virtue of which they can appear visibly as the rulers. This would be ridiculous and senseless. It is much more the recognition on the part of the lower ones that is the true basis of any traditional ranking. It is not the higher that needs the lower, but the other way round. The essence of hierarchy is that there is something living as a reality in certain people, which in the rest is only present in the condition of an ideal, a premonition, an unfocused effort. Thus the latter are fatefully attracted to the former, and their lower condition is one of subordination less to something foreign, than to their own true "self." Herein lies the secret, in the traditional world, of all readiness for sacrifice, all heroism, all loyalty; and, on the other side, of a prestige, an authority, and a calm power which the most heavily-armed tyrant can never count upon.

With these considerations, we have come very close to solving not only the problem of degeneration, but also the possibility of a particular fall. Are we perhaps not tired of hearing that the success of every revolution indicates the weakness and degeneracy of the previous rulers? An understanding of this kind is very one-sided. This would indeed be the case if wild dogs were tied up, and suddenly broke loose: that would be proof that the hands holding their leashes had become impotent or weak. But things are arranged very differently in the framework of spiritual ranking, whose real basis we have explained above. This hierarchy degenerates and is able to be overthrown in one case only: when the individual degenerates, when he uses his fundamental freedom to deny the Spirit, to cut his life loose from any higher reference-point, and to exist "only for himself." Then the contacts are fatefully broken, the metaphysical tension, to which the traditional organism owes its unity, gives way, every force wavers in its path and finally breaks free. The peaks, of course, remain pure and inviolable in their heights, but the rest, which depended on them, now becomes an avalanche, a mass that has lost its equilibrium and falls, at first imperceptibly but with ever accelerating movement down to the depths and lowest levels of the valley. This is the secret of every degeneration and revolution. The European had first slain the hierarchy in himself by extirpating his own inner possibilities, to which corresponded the basis of the order that he would then destroy externally. If Christian mythology attributes the Fall of Man and the Rebellion of the Angels to the freedom of the will, then it comes to much the same significance. It concerns the frightening potential that dwells in man of using freedom to destroy spiritually and to banish everything that could ensure him a supra-natural value. This is a metaphysical decision: the stream that traverses history in the most varied forms of the traditional-hating, revolutionary, individualistic, and humanistic spirit, or in short, the "modern" spirit. This decision is the only positive and decisive cause in the secret of degeneration, the destruction of Tradition.

If we understand this, we can perhaps also grasp the sense of those legends that speak of mysterious rulers who "always" exist and have never died (shades of the Emperor sleeping beneath the Kyffhäuser mountain!). Such rulers can be rediscovered only when one achieves spiritual completeness and awakens a quality in oneself like that of a metal that suddenly feels "the magnet", finds the magnet and irresistibly orients itself and moves towards it. For now, we must restrict ourselves to this hint. A comprehensive explanation of legends of that sort, which come to us from the most ancient Aryan source, would take us too far. At another opportunity we will perhaps return to the secret of reconstruction, to the "magic" that is capable of restoring the fallen mass to the unalterable, lonely, and invisible peaks that are still there in the heights.

American "Civilization"

The recently deceased John Dewey was applauded by the American press as the most representative figure of American civilisation. This is quite right. His theories are entirely representative of the vision of man and life which is the premise of Americanism and its 'democracy'.

The essence of such theories is this: that everyone can become what he wants to, within the limits of the technological means at his disposal. Equally, a person is not what he is from his true nature and there is no real difference between people, only differences in qualifications. According to this theory anyone can be anyone he wants to be if he knows how to train himself. This is obviously the case with the 'self-made man'; in a society which has lost all sense of tradition the notion of personal aggrandizement will extend into every aspect of human existence, reinforcing the egalitarian doctrine of pure democracy. If the basis of such ideas is accepted, then all natural diversity has to be abandoned. Each person can presume to possess the potential of everyone else and the terms 'superior' and 'inferior' lose their meaning; every notion of distance and respect loses meaning; all life-styles are open to all. To all organic conceptions of life Americans oppose a mechanistic conception. In a society which has 'started from scratch', everything has the characteristic of being fabricated. In American society appearances are masks not faces. At the same time, proponents of the American way of life are hostile to personality.

The Americans' 'open-mindedness', which is sometimes cited in their favour, is the other side of their interior formlessness. The same goes for their 'individualism'. Individualism and personality are not the same: the one belongs to the formless world of quantity, the other to the world of quality and hierarchy. The Americans are the living refutation of the Cartesian axiom, "I think, therefore I am": Americans do not think, yet they are. The American 'mind', puerile and primitive, lacks characteristic form and is therefore open to every kind of standardization In a superior civilization, as, for example, that of the Indo-Aryans, the being who is without a characteristic form or caste (in the original meaning of the word), not even that of servant or shudra, would emerge as a pariah. In this respect America is a society of pariahs. There is a role for pariahs. It is to be subjected to beings whose form and internal laws are precisely defined. Instead the modern pariahs seek to become dominant themselves and to exercise their dominion over all the world. There is a popular notion about the United States that it is a 'young nation' with a 'great future before it'. Apparent American defects are then described as the 'faults of youth' or 'growing pains'. It is not difficult to see that the myth of 'progress' plays a large part in this judgment. According to the idea that everything new is good, America has a privileged role to play among civilized nations. In the First World War the United States intervened in the role of 'the civilised world' par excellence. The 'most evolved' nation had not only a right but a duty to interfere in the destinies of other peoples.

The structure of history is, however, cyclical not evolutionary. It is far from being the case that the most recent civilizations are necessarily 'superior'. They may be, in fact, senile and decadent.

There is a necessary correspondence between the most advanced stages of a historical cycle and the most primitive. America is the final stage of modern Europe. Guenon called the United States 'the far West', in the novel sense that the United States represents the reductio ad absurdum of the negative and the most senile aspects of Western civilization. What in Europe exist in diluted form are magnified and concentrated in the United States whereby they are revealed as the symptoms of disintegration and cultural and human regression.

The American mentality can only be interpreted as an example of regression, which shows itself in the mental atrophy towards all higher interests and incomprehension of higher sensibility. The American mind has limited horizons, one conscribed to the very thing which is immediate and simplistic, with the inevitable consequence that everything is made banal, basic and leveled down until it is deprived of all spiritual life. Life itself in American terms is entirely mechanistic. The sense of 'I' in America belongs entirely to the physical level of existence. The typical American neither has spiritual dilemmas nor complications: he is a 'natural' joiner and conformist. The primitive American mind can only superficially be compared to a young mind. The American mind is a feature of the regressive society to which I have already referred.

American Morality

The much-vaunted sex appeal of American women is drawn from films, reviews and pin-ups, and is in large print fictitious. A recent medical survey in the United States showed that 75 per cent of young American women are without strong sexual feeling and instead of satisfying their libido they seek pleasure narcissistically in exhibitionism, vanity and the cult of fitness and health in a sterile sense. American girls have 'no hang-ups about sex'; they are 'easy going' for the man who sees the whole sexual process as something in isolation thereby making it uninteresting and matter-of-fact, which, at such a level, it is meant to be. Thus, after she has been taken to the cinema or a dance, it is something like American good manners for the girl to let herself be kissed - this doesn't mean anything. American women are characteristically frigid and materialistic. The man who 'has his way' with an American girl is under a material obligation to her. The woman has granted a material favour. In cases of divorce American law overwhelmingly favors the woman. American women will divorce readily enough when they see a better bargain. It is frequently the case in America that a woman will be married to one man but already 'engaged' to a future husband, the man she plans to marry after a profitable divorce.

"Our" American Media

Americanization in Europe is widespread and evident. In Italy it is a phenomenon which is rapidly developing in these post-war years and is considered by most people, if not enthusiastically, at least as something natural. Some time ago I wrote that of the two great dangers confronting Europe - Americanism and Communism - the first is the more insidious. Communism cannot be a danger other than in the brutal and catastrophic form of a direct seizure of power by communists. On the other hand Americanization gains ground by a process of gradual infiltration, effecting modifications of mentalities and customs which seem inoffensive in themselves but which end in a fundamental perversion and degradation against which it is impossible to fight other than within oneself. It is precisely with respect to such internal opposition that most Italians seem weak. Forgetting their own cultural inheritance they readily turn to the United States as something akin to the parent guide of the world. Whoever wants to be modern has to measure himself according to the American standard. It is pitiable to witness a European country so debase itself. Veneration for America has nothing to do with a cultured interest in the way other people live. On the contrary, servility towards the United States leads one to think that there is no other way of life worth considering on the same level as the American one.

Our radio service is Americanized. Without any criterion of superior and inferior it just follows the fashionable themes of the moment and markets what is considered 'acceptable' – acceptable, that is, to the most Americanized section of the public, which is to say the most degenerate. The rest of us are dragged along in its wake. Even the style of presentation on radio has become Americanized "Who, after listening to an American radio program, can suppress a shudder when he considers that the only way of escaping communism is by becoming Americanized?" Those are not the words of an outsider but of an American sociologist, James Burnham, professor at the University of Princeton. Such a judgment from an American should make Italian radio programmers blush for shame.

The consequence of the 'do your own thing' democracy is the intoxication of the greater part of the population which is not capable of discriminating for itself, which, when not guided by a power and an ideal, all too easily loses sense of its own identity.

The Industrial Order in America

In his classic study of capitalism Werner Sombart summarized the late capitalist phase in the adage Fiat producto, pareat homo. In its extreme form capitalism is a system in which a man's value is estimated solely in terms of the production of merchandise and the invention of the means of production. Socialist doctrines grew out of a reaction to the lack of human consideration in this system. A new phase has begun in the United States where there has been an upsurge of interest in so called labor relations. In appearance it would seem to signify an improvement; in reality this is a deleterious phenomenon. The entrepreneurs and employers have come to realize the importance of the 'human factor' in a productive economy, and that it is a mistake to ignore the individual involved in industry: his motives, his feelings, his working day life. Thus, a whole school of study of human relations in industry has grown up, based on behaviorism. Studies like Human Relations in Industry by B. Gardner and G. Moore have supplied a minute analysis of the behavior of employees and their motivations with the precise aim of defining the best means to obviate all factors that can hinder the maximization of production. Some studies certainly don't come from the shop floor but from the management, abetted by specialists from various colleges. The sociological investigations go as far! as analyzing the employee's social ambiance. This kind of study has a practical purpose: the maintenance of the psychological contentment of the employee is as important as the physical. In cases in which a worker is tied to a monotonous job which doesn't demand a great deal of concentration, the studies will draw attention to the 'danger' that his mind may tend to wander in a way that may eventually reflect badly on his attitude towards the job. The private lives of employees are not forgotten – hence the increase in so-called personnel counseling. Specialists are called in to dispel anxiety, psychological disturbances and non adaptation 'complexes', even to the point of giving advice in relation to the most personal matters. A frankly psycho-analytic technique and one much used is to make the subject 'talk freely' and put the results obtainable by this 'catharsis' into relief.

None of this is concerned with the spiritual betterment of human beings or any real human problems, such as a European would understand them in this "age of economics". On the other side of the Iron Curtain man is treated as a beast of burden and his obedience is maintained by terror and famine. In the United States man is also seen as just a factor of labour and consumption, and no aspect of his interior life is neglected and every factor of his existence is drawn to the same end. In the 'Land of the Free', through every medium, man is told he has reached a degree of happiness hitherto undreamed of. He forgets who he is, where he came from, and basks in the present.

American "Democracy" in Industry

There is a significant and growing discrepancy in the United States between the shibboleths of the prevailing political ideology and the effective economic structures of the nation. A large part of studies of the subject is played by the 'morphology of business'. Studies corroborate the impression that American business is a long way from the type of organization which corresponds to the democratic ideal of U.S. propaganda. American businesses have a 'pyramid' structure. They constitute at the top an articulate hierarchy. The big businesses are run in the same way as government ministries and are organized along similar lines. They have coordinating and controlling bodies which separate the business leaders from the mass of employees. Rather than becoming more flexible in a social sense the "managerial elite" (Burnham) is becoming more autocratic than ever – something not unrelated to American foreign policy.

This is the end of yet another American illusion. America: the 'land of opportunity', where every possibility is there for the person who can grasp it, a land where anyone can rise from rags to riches. At first there was the 'open frontier' for all to ride out across. That closed and the new 'open frontier' was the sky, the limitless potential of industry and commerce. As Gardner, Moore and many others have shown, this too is no longer limitless, and the opportunities are thinning out. Given the ever increasing specialization of labour in the productive process and the increasing emphasis on 'qualifications', what used to seem obvious to Americans – that their children would 'go further' than they would – is for many people no longer obvious at all. Thus it is that in the so-called political democracy of the United States, the force and the power in the land, that is to say the industry and the economy, are becoming ever more self-evidently undemocratic. The problem then is! : should reality be made to fit ideology or vice-versa? Until recently the overwhelming demand has been for the former course of action; the cry goes out for a return to the 'real America' of unfettered enterprise and the individual free of central government control. Nevertheless, there are also those who would prefer to limit democracy in order to adapt political theory to commercial reality. If the mask of American 'democracy' were thereby removed, it would become clear to what extent 'democracy' in America (and elsewhere) is only the instrument of an oligarchy which pursues a method of 'indirect action', assuring the possibility of abuse and deception on a large scale of those many who accept a hierarchical system because they think it is justly such. This dilemma of 'democracy' in the United States may one day give place to some interesting developments.

Against the Neo-Pagans

The Misunderstandings of the New "Paganism"

It is perhaps appropriate to point out the misunderstandings that are current at the moment in some radical circles, who believe that a solution lies in the direction of a new paganism. This misunderstanding is already visible in the use of terms such as "pagan" and "pagandom". I myself, having used these expressions as slogans in a book that was published in Italy in 1928, and in Germany in 1934, have cause for sincere regrets. Certainly the word for pagan or heathen, paganus, appears in some ancient Latin writers such as Livy without an especially negative tone. But this does not alter the fact that with the arrival of the new faith, the word paganus became a decidedly disparaging expression, as used in early Christian apologetics. It derives from pagus, meaning a small town or village, so that paganus refers to the peasant way of thinking: an uncultured, primitive, and superstitious way. In order to promote and glorify the new faith, the apologists had the bad habit of elevating themselves through the denigration of other faiths. There was often a conscious and often systematic disparagement and misrepresentation of almost all the earlier traditions, doctrines, and religions, which were grouped under the contemptuous blanket-term of paganism or heathendom. To this end, the apologists obviously made a premeditated effort to highlight those aspects of the pre-Christian religions and traditions that lacked any normal or primordial character, but were clearly forms that had fallen into decay. Such a polemical procedure lead, in particular, to the characterization of whatever had preceded Christendom, and was hence non-Christian, as necessarily anti-Christian. One should consider, then, that "paganism" is a fundamentally tendentious and artificial concept that scarcely corresponds to the historical reality of what the pre-Christian world always was in its normal manifestations, apart from a few decadent elements and aspects that derived from the degenerate remains of older cultures.

Once we are clear about this, we come today to a paradoxical realization: that this imaginary paganism that never existed, but was invented by Christian apologists, is now serving as the starting-point for certain so-called pagan circles, and is thus threatening for the first time in history to become a reality--no more and no less than that. What are the main traits of today's pagan outlook, as its own apologists believe and declare them to be? The primary one is the imprisonment in Nature. All transcendence is totally unknown to the pagan view of life: it remains stuck in a mixture of Spirit and Nature, in an ambiguous unity of Body and Soul. There is nothing to its religion but a superstitious deification of natural phenomena, or of tribal energies promoted to the status of minor gods. Out of this there arises first of all a blood- and soil-bound particularism. Next comes a rejection of the values of personality and freedom, and a condition of innocence that is merely that of the natural man, as yet unawakened to any truly supra-natural calling. Beyond this innocence there is only lack of inhibition, "sin," and the pleasure of sinning. In other domains there is nothing but superstition, or a purely profane culture of materialism and fatalism. It is as though only the arrival of Christianity (ignoring certain precursors which are dismissed as insignificant) allowed the world of supra-natural freedom to break through, letting in grace and personality, in contrast to the fatalistic and nature-bound beliefs ascribed to "paganism," bringing with it a catholic ideal (in the etymological sense of universality) and a healthy dualism, which made it possible to subjugate Nature to a higher law, and for the "Spirit" to triumph over the law of flesh, blood, and the false gods.

These are the main traits of the dominant understanding of paganism, i.e., of everything that does not entail a specifically Christian world-view. Anyone who possesses any direct acquaintance with cultural and religious history, however elementary, can see how incorrect and one-sided this attitude is. Besides, in the early Church Fathers there are often signs of a higher understanding of the symbols, doctrines, and religions of preceding cultures. Here we will give only a sampling.

What most distinguished the pre-Christian world, in all its normal forms, was not the superstitious divinization of nature, but a symbolic understanding of it, by virtue of which (as I have often emphasized) every phenomenon and every event appeared as the sensible revelation of a supra-sensible world. The pagan understanding of the world and of man was essentially marked by sacred symbolism.

Moreover, the pagan way of life was absolutely not that of a mindless innocence, nor a natural abandonment to the passions, even if certain forms of it were obviously degenerate. It was already aware of a healthy dualism, which is reflected in its universal religious or metaphysical conceptions. Here we can mention the dualistic warrior-religion of the ancient Iranian Aryans, already discussed and familiar to all; the Hellenistic antithesis between the "two natures," between World and

Underworld, or the Nordic one between the race of the Ases and the elementary beings; and lastly the Indo-Aryan contrast between sams'ra, the "stream of forms," and m(o)kthi, "liberation" and "perfection."

On this basis, all the great pre-Christian cultures shared the striving for a supra-natural freedom, i.e., for the metaphysical perfection of the personality, and they all acknowledged Mysteries and initiations. I have already pointed out that the Mysteries often signified the reconquest of the primordial state, the spirituality of the solar, Hyperborean races, on the foundation of a tradition and a knowledge that were concealed through secrecy and exclusivity from the pollutions of an environment already in decay. We have also seen that in the Eastern lands, the Aryan quality was already associated with a "second birth" achieved through initiation. As for natural innocence as the pagan cult of the body, that is a fairy-tale and not even in evidence among savages, for despite the inner lack of differentiation already mentioned in connection with races "close to nature," these people inhibit and constrict their lives though countless taboos in a way that is often stricter than the morality of the so-called "positive religions." And as for that which seems to the superficial view to embody the prototype of such "innocence," namely the classical ideal, that was no cult of the body: it did not belong on that side of the body-spirit duality, but on the other side. As already stated, the classic ideal is that of a Spirit that is so dominant that under certain favorable spiritual conditions it molds Body and Soul to its own image, and thereby achieves a perfect harmony between the inner and the outer.

Lastly, there is an aspiration away from particularism to be found everywhere in the "pagan" world, to which was due the imperial summons that marked the ascending phase of the Nordic derived races. Such a summons was often metaphysically enhanced and refined, and appeared as the natural consequence of the expansion of the ancient sacred state-concept; also as the form in which the victorious presence of the "higher world" and the paternal, Olympian principle sought to manifest itself in the world of becoming. In this respect we might recall the old Iranian concept of Empire and of the "King of kings," with its associated doctrine of the hvarenÙ (the "celestial glory" with which the Aryan rulers were endowed), and the Indo-Aryan tradition of the "World-king" or cakravartÓ, etc., right up to the reappearance of these signifiers in the "Olympian" assumptions of the ancient Roman idea of State and Empire.

The Roman Empire, too, had its sacred contents, which were systematically misunderstood or undervalued not only by Christendom, but also by the writers of "positive" history. Even the Emperor-cult had the sense of a hierarchical unity at the top of a pantheon, which was a series of separate territorial and ancestral cults belonging to the non-Roman peoples, which were freely respected so long as they kept within their normal boundaries. Finally, concerning the "pagan" unity of the two powers, spiritual and temporal, this was very far from meaning that they were fused As a "solar" race understood it, it expressed the superior rights that must accrue to the spiritual authority at the center of any normal state; thus it was something quite different from the emancipation and "supremacy" of a merely secular state. If we were to make similar amendments in the spirit of true objectivity, the possibilities would be overwhelming.

Further Misunderstandings Concerning the "Pagan" World-View

This having been said, there remains the real possibility of transcending certain aspects of Christianity. But one must be quite clear: the Latin term "*transcendere*" means literally leaving something behind as one rises upwards, and not downwards! It is worth repeating that the principal thing is not the rejection of Christianity: it is not a matter of showing the same incomprehension towards it as Christianity itself has shown, and largely continues to show, towards ancient paganism. It would rather be a matter of completing Christianity by means of a higher and an older heritage, eliminating some of its aspects and emphasizing other, more important ones, in which this faith does not necessarily contradict the universal concepts of pre-Christian spirituality. This, alas, is not the path taken by the radical circles we have mentioned. Many of these neopagans seem to have fallen into a trap deliberately set for them, often ending up by advocating and defending ideas that more or less correspond to that invented, nature-bound, particularistic pagandom, lacking light and transcendence, which was the polemical creation of a Christian misunderstanding of the pre-Christian world, and which is based, at most, on a few scattered elements of that world in its decline and devolution. And as if this were not enough, people often resort to an anti-Catholic polemic which, whatever its political justification, often drags out and adapts the old clichès of a purely modern, rationalist and enlightenment type that have been well-used by Liberalism, Democracy, and Freemasonry. This was also the case, to a degree, with H. S. Chamberlain, and it appears again in a certain Italian movement that has been trying to connect racial thinking with the "idealistic" doctrine of immanence.

There is a general and unmistakable tendency in neo-paganism to create a new, superstitious mysticism, based on the glorification of immanence, of Life and Nature, which is in the sharpest contrast to that Olympian and heroic ideal of the great Aryan cultures of pre-Christian antiquity. It would indicate much more a turning towards the materialistic, maternal, and telluric side, if it did not exhaust itself in foggy and dilettantish philosophizing. To give an example, we might ask what exactly is meant by this "Nature," on which these groups are so keen? It is little use to point out that it is certainly not the Nature that was experienced and recognized by ancient, traditional man, but a rational construct of the French Encyclopedist period. It was the Encyclopedists who, with definitely subversive and revolutionary motives, made up the myth of Nature as "good," wise, and wholesome, in opposition to the rottenness of every human "Culture." Thus we can see that the optimistic nature-myth of Rousseau and the Encyclopedists marches in the same ranks as "natural right," universalism, liberalism, humanitarianism, and the denial of any positive and structured form of sovereignty. Moreover, the myth in question has absolutely no basis in natural history. Every honest scientist knows that there is no room for "Nature" in the framework of his theories, which have as their object the determination of purely abstract equivalences and mathematical relationships. As far as biological research and genetics are concerned, we can already see the disequilibrium that would occur the moment one held certain laws to be final, when they only apply to a partial aspect of reality. What people call "Nature" today has nothing to do with what nature meant to the traditional, solar man, or to the knowledge of it that was accessible to such a man thanks to his Olympian and regal position. There is no sign of this whatever in the advocates of this new mysticism.

Misunderstandings of more or less the same kind. arise regarding political thought. Paganism is here often used as the synonym for a merely worldly and yet exclusive concept of sovereignty, which turns the relationships upside-down. We have already seen that in the ancient states, the unity of the two powers meant something quite different. It provided the basis for the spiritualization of politics, whereas neo-paganism results in actually politicizing the spiritual, and thereby treading once again the false path of the Gallicans and Jacobins. In contrast, the ancient concept of State and Empire always showed a connection to the Olympian idea. What shall we think of the attitude that regards Jewry, Rome, the Catholic Church, Freemasonry, and Communism as more or less one and the same thing, just because their presuppositions differ from the plain thinking of the Folk? The Folk's thinking along these lines threatens to lose itself in the dark, where no differentiation is possible any more. It shows that it has lost the genuine feeling for the hierarchy of values, and that it cannot escape the crippling alternative of destructive internationalism and nationalistic particularism, whereas the traditional understanding of the Empire is superior to both these concepts.

To restrict ourselves to a single example: Catholic dogmatism actually fulfills a useful preventive role by stopping worldly mysticism and suchlike eruptions from below from passing a certain frontier; it makes a strong dam that protects the area where transcendent knowledge and the genuinely supra-natural and non-human elements reign--or at least where they should reign. One may well criticize the way in which such transcendence and knowledge have been understood in Christianity, but one cannot cross over to a "profane" criticism that seizes on some polemical weapon or other, fantasizes over the supposed Aryan nature of the immanence-doctrine, of "natural religion," the cult of "life," etc., without really losing one's level: in short, one does not thereby attain the world of primordial beginnings, but that of the Counter-Tradition or the telluric and primitive modes of being. This would in fact be the very best way of re-converting those people with the best "pagan" talents to Catholicism! One must be wary of falling into the misunderstandings and errors that we have mentioned, which basically serve only to defend the common enemy. One must try to develop the capacity to place oneself at that level where didactic confusion cannot reach, and where all dilettantism and arbitrary intellectual activity are excluded; where one resists energetically every influence from confused, passionate desires and from the aggressive pleasure in polemics; where, finally and fundamentally, nothing counts but the precise, strict, objective knowledge of the spirit of the Primordial Tradition.

The Meaning and Context of Zen

We know the kind of interest Zen has evoked even outside specialized disciplines, since being popularized in the west by D.T. Suzuki through his books *Introduction to Zen Buddhism* and *Essays in Zen Buddhism*. This popular interest is due to the paradoxical encounter between East and West. The ailing West perceives that Zen has something "existential" and surrealistic to offer. Zen's notion of a spiritual realization, free from any faith and any bond, not to mention the mirage of an instantaneous and somehow gratuitous "spiritual breakthrough", has exercised a fascinating attraction on many Westerners. However, this is true, for the most part, only superficially. There is a considerable difference between the spiritual dimension of the "philosophy of crisis", which has become popular in the West as a consequence of its materialistic and nihilist development, and the spiritual dimension of Zen, which has been rooted in the spirituality of the Buddhist tradition. Any true encounter between Zen and the West, presupposes, in a Westerner, either an exceptional predisposition, or the capability to operate a *metanoia*. By *metanoia* I mean an inner turnabout, affecting not so much one's intellectual "attitudes", but rather a dimension which in every time and in every place has been conceived as a deeper reality.

Zen has a secret doctrine and not to be found in scriptures. It was passed on by the Buddha to his disciple Mahakassapa. This secret doctrine was introduced in China around the sixth century C.E. by Bodhidharma. The canon was transmitted in China and Japan through a succession on teachers and "patriarchs". In Japan it is a living tradition and has many advocates and numerous *Zendos* ("Halls of Meditation").

As far as the spirit informing the tradition is concerned, Zen may be considered as a continuation of early Buddhism. Buddhism arose as a vigorous reaction against the theological speculation and the shallow ritualism into which the ancient Hindu priestly caste had degraded after possessing a sacred, lively wisdom since ancient times. Buddha made *tabula rasa* of all this: he focused instead on the practical problem of how to overcome what in the popular mind is referred to as "life's suffering". According to esoteric teachings, this suffering was considered as the state of caducity, restlessness, "thirst" and the forgetfulness typical of ordinary people. Having followed the path leading to spiritual awakening and to immortality without external aid, Buddha pointed the way to those who felt an attraction to it. It is well known that Buddha is not a name, but an attribute or a title meaning "the awakened One", "He who has achieved enlightenment", or "the awakening". Buddha was silent about the content of his experience, since he wanted to discourage people from assigning to speculation and philosophizing a primacy over action. Therefore, unlike his predecessors, he did not talk about *Brahman* (the absolute), or about *Atman* (the transcendental Self), but only employees the term *nirvana*, at the risk of bein misunderstood. Some, in fact, thought, in their lack of understanding, that *nirvana* was to be identified with the notion of "nothingness", an ineffable and evanescent transcendence, almost bordering on the limits of the unconscious and of a state of unaware non-being. So, in a further development of Buddhism, what occurred again, *mutatis mutandi*, was exactly the situation against which Buddha had reacted; Buddhism became a religion, complete with dogmas, rituals, scholasticism and mythology. It eventually became differentiated into two schools: *Mahayana* and *Hinayana*. The former was more grandiose in metaphysics an *Mahayana* eventually grew complacent with its abstruse symbolism. The teachings of the latter school were more strict and to the point, and yet too concerned about the mere moral discipline which became increasingly monastic. Thus the essential and original nucleus, namely the esoteric doctrine of the enlightenment, was almost lost.

At this crucial time Zen appeared, declaring the uselessness of these so-called methods and proclaiming the doctrine of *satori*. *Satori* is a fundamental inner event, a sudden existential breakthrough, corresponding in essence to what I have called the "awakening". But this formulation was new and original and it constituted a radical change in approach. *Nirvana*, which had been variously considered as the alleged Nothingness, as extinction, and as the final end result of an effort aimed at obtaining liberation (which according to some may require more than one lifetime), now came to be considered as the normal human condition. By these lights, every person has the nature of Buddha and every person is already liberated, and therefore, situated above and beyond birth and death. It is only necessary to become aware of it, to realize it, to see within one's nature, according to Zen's main expression. *Satori* is like a timeless opening up. On the one hand, *satori* is something sudden and radically different from all the ordinary human states of consciousness; it is like a catastrophic trauma within ordinary consciousness. On the other hand, *satori* is what leads one back to what, in a higher sense, should be considered as normal and natural; thus, it is the exact opposite of an ecstasy, or trance. It is the rediscovery and the appropriation of one's true nature; it is the enlightenment which draws out of ignorance or out of the subconscious the deep reality of what was and will always be, regardless of one's condition in life. The consequence of *satori* is a completely new way to look at the world and at life. To those who have experienced it, everything is the same (things, other beings, one's self, "heaven, the rivers and the vast earth"), and yet everything is fundamentally different. It is as if a new dimension was added to reality, transforming the meaning and value. According to the Zen Masters, the essential characteristic of the new experience is the overcoming of every dualism: of the inner and outer; the I and not I; of finitude and infinity; being and not-being; appearance and reality; "empty" and "full"; substance and accidents. Another characteristic is that any value posed by the finite and confused consciousness of the individual, is no longer discernible. And thus, the liberated and the non-liberated, the enlightened and the non-enlightened, are yet one and same thing. Zen effectively perpetuates the paradoxical equation of *Mahayana* Buddhism, *nirvana-samsara*, and the Taoist saying "the return is infinitely far". It is as if Zen said: liberation should not be looked for in the next world; the very world is the next world; it is liberation and it does not need to be liberated. This is the point of view of *satori*, of perfect enlightenment, of "transcendent wisdom" (*prajnaparamita*). Basically, this consciousness is a shift of the self's center. In any situation and in any event of ordinary life, including the most trivial ones, the ordinary, dualistic and intellectual sense of one's self is substituted with a being who no longer perceives an "I" opposed to a "non-I", and who transcends and overcomes any antithesis. This being eventually comes to enjoy a perfect freedom an incoercibility. He is like the wind, which blows where it wills, and like a naked being which is everything after "letting go" -abandons everything, embracing poverty.

Zen, or at least mainstream Zen, emphasizes the discontinuous, sudden and unpredictable character of *satori* disclosure. In regard to this, Suzuki was at fault when he took issue with the techniques used in Hindu schools such as *Samkya* and *Yoga*. These techniques were also contemplated in early Buddhist texts. Suzuki employed the simile of water, which in a moment turns into ice. He also used the simile of an alarm, which, as a consequence of some vibration, suddenly goes off. There are no disciplines, techniques or efforts, according to Suzuki, which by themselves may lead one to *satori*. On the contrary, it is claimed that *satori* often occurs spontaneously, when one has exhausted all the resources of his being, especially the intellect and logical faculty of understanding. In some cases satori it is said to be facilitated by violent sensations and even by physical pain. Its cause may be the mere perception of an object as well as any event in ordinary life, provided a certain latent predisposition exists in the subject.

Regarding this, some misunderstandings may occur. Suzuki acknowledged that *"generally peaking, there are no indications on the inner work preceding satori"*. However, he talked about the necessity of first going through *"a true baptism of fire"*. After all, the very institution of the so-called "Halls of Meditation" (*Zendo*), where those who strive to obtain a *satori* submit themselves to a regimen of life which is partially analogous to that of some Catholic religious orders, bespeaks the necessity of a preliminary preparation. This preparation may last for several years. The essence of Zen seems to consist in a maturation process, identical to the one in which one almost reaches a state of an acute existential instability. At that point, the slightest push is sufficient to produce a change of state, a spiritual breakthrough, the opening which leads to the "*intuitive vision of one's nature*". The Masters know the moment in which the mind of the disciple is mature and ready to open up; it is ten that they eventually give the final. Decisive push. This push may sometimes consist of a simple gesture, an exclamation, in something apparently irrelevant, or even illogical and absurd. This suffices to induce the collapse of the false notion of individuality. Thus, *satori* replaces this notion with the "*normal state*", and one assumes the "*original face, which one had before creation*". One no longer "*chases after echoes*" and "*shadows*". This under some aspects brings to mind the existential theme of "failure", or of "being shipwrecked" (*das Scheitern*, in Kierkegaard and in Jaspers). In fact, as I have mentioned, the opening often takes place when all the resources of one's being have been exhausted and one has his back against the wall. This can be seen in relation to some practical teachings methods used by Zen. The most frequently employed methods, on an intellectual plane, are the *koan* and the *mondo*. The disciple is confronted with a saying or with questions which are paradoxical, absurd and sometimes even grotesque and "surrealistic". He must labor with his mind, if necessary for years, until he has reached the extreme limit of all his normal faculties of comprehension. Then, if he dares proceed further on that road he may find catastrophe, but if he can turn the situation upside down, he may achieve *metanoia*. This is the point where *satori* is usually achieved.

Zen's norm is that of absolute autonomy; no gods, no cults, no idols. To literally empty oneself of everything, including God. *"If you meet Buddha on the road, kill him"*, a saying goes. It is necessary to abandon everything, without leaning on anything, and then to proceed forward, with one's essence, until the crisis point is reached. It is very difficult to say more about satori, or to compare it with various forms of initiatory mystical experience whether Eastern or Western. One is supposed to spend only the training period in Zen monasteries. Once the disciple has achieved *satori*, he return to the world, choosing a way of life that fits his need. One may think of *satori* as a form of transcendence which is brought to immanence, as a natural state, in every form of life. The behavior which proceeds from the newly acquired dimension, which is added to reality as a consequence of *satori*, may well be summarized by Lao Tzu's expression: *"To be the whole in the part"*. In regard to this, it is important to realize the influence which Zen has exercised on the Far-Eastern way of life. Zen has been called "the samurai's philosophy," and it had also been said that "the way of Zen is identical to the way of archery," or to the "way of the sword". This means that any activity in one's life, may be permeated by Zen and thus be elevated to a higher meaning, to a "wholesomeness" and to an "impersonal activity". This kind of activity is based on a sense of the individual's irrelevance, which nevertheless does not paralyze one's actions, but which rather confers cam and detachment. This detachment, in turn, favors an absolute and "pure" undertaking of life, which in some cases reaches extreme and distinct forms of self sacrifice and heroism, inconceivable to the majority of Westerners (e.g. the *kamikaze* in WWII). Thus, what C.G. Jung claims is simply ridiculous, namely that Psychoanalysis, more than any other Western school of thought, is capable of understanding Zen. According to Jung, *satori* coincides with the state of wholeness, devoid of complexes or inner splitting, which psychoanalytic treatment claims to achieve whenever the intellect's obstructions and its sense of superiority are removed, and whenever the conscious dimension of the soul is reunited with the unconscious and with "Life". Jung did not realize that the methods and presuppositions of Zen, are exactly the opposite of his own. There is no "subconscious", as a distinct entity, to which the conscious has to be reconnected; Zen speaks of a superconscious vision (enlightenment, *bodhi* or "awakening"), which actualizes the "original and luminous nature" and which, in so doing, destroys the unconscious. It is possible though, to notice similarities between Jung's view's and Zen', since they both talk about the feeling of one's "totality" and freedom which is manifested in every aspect of life. However, it is important to explain the level at which these views appear to coincide. Once Zen found its way to the West, there was a tendency to "domesticate" and to moralize it, playing down its potential radical and "antinomian" (namely, antithetical to current norms) implications, and by emphasizing the standard ingredients which are held so dear by "spiritual" people, namely love and service to one's neighbor, even though these ingredients have been purified in an impersonal and non-sentimental form. Generally speaking, there are many doubts on the "practicability" o f Zen, considering that the "doctrine of the awakening" has an initiatory character.

Thus, it will only be able to inspire a minority of people, in contrast to later Buddhist views, which took the form of a religion open to everyone, for the most part a code of mere morality. As the reestablishment of the spirit of early Buddhism, Zen should have strictly been an esoteric doctrine. It has been so as we can see by examining the legend concerning its origins. However, Suzuki himself was inclined to give a different account; he emphasized those aspects of *Mahayana* which "democratize" Buddhism (after all, the term *Mahayana* has been interpreted to mean "Great Vehicle", even in the sense that it extends to wider audiences, and not just to a few elect). If one was to fully agree with Suzuki, some perplexities on the nature and on the scope of *satori* may arise. One should ask whether such an experience merely affects the psychological, moral or mental domain, or whether it affects the ontological domain, as is the case in every authentic initiation. In that event, it can only be the privilege a very restricted number of people.

Yoga, Immortality and Freedom

Yoga, may well he said to be that portion of the heritage of Indian wisdom—nay, of the wisdom of the East as a whole—that is most familiar to Western Europeans and to Americans. Even newspaper readers and readers of popular fiction of the Somerset Maugham type, have an idea—confused though it may be—of Yoga and the yogis. Ever since the opening of the century they have attracted the attention of the West. And here it should be noted that at first, rather than of the serious studies made by Oriental scholars, it has been a question of superficial works written less with a view to making the theory known, than for acquainting the reader with the techniques followed to secure results on the spiritual plane and to produce supernormal phenomena. It is known that among these popularizers a foremost place is held by Ramacharaka, the pseudonym used by an American. His works however have often been mere profanations and distortions. The real substance and final aims of Yoga are often set aside in favor of commonplace applications and adaptations such as physical training, psychic training, the secret of success, deep breathing as a branch of hygiene, mental treatment of disease, Americanized Yoga, and so forth.

Perhaps still more regrettable has been the insertion of Yoga in a vaguely spiritualized framework or in a purely fanciful one. In this field the record has been beaten by the *Autobiography of a Yogi*, by Yogananda, a book on the level of fairy tales for children which in the West has scored a bookselling success and has been translated into several languages. As Yogananda is a Hindu, it should be noted that the spate of Western popularizers and adapters has been followed by another of writers exported from India, attracted abroad by the environment prepared by the Western popularizers. This second group has given rise to a dangerous misunderstanding. Persons lacking the knowledge required for discriminating have thought that the mere fact of being a Hindu sufficed to make a man an authority on Hindu doctrines. Now, for intrinsic reasons due to the essentially esoteric nature of real Yoga, there is good reason to presume that those Orientals who feel the need of popularizing such doctrines and who become, so to speak, commercial travelers, peddling their goods in the West, can only be spurious exponents of their traditions. The same may be said of some Indians who have made themselves readily "accessible" as "masters" in their own country, opening study centers, sometimes provided with typist, an administrative department, a correspondence bureau, etc. As a result of this, it often happens that those Westerners who have succeeded in penetrating and illustrating the real essence of the traditional wisdom of India are asked if they have not been engaged in the construction of some abstract ideal of their own, so different is the level of the teachings they impart to that of the authentic Indians of our day who have become the exporters and vulgarizers of the ancient wisdom. It is only recently that scientific studies on Yoga by Westerners are keeping pace with those works of divulgation, as contributions in the domain of orientalism and the history of religions. But here we meet with the obstacle created by the "objective method" which aims at an exclusively exterior, documentary, and informative exactness. It is like undertaking the study of the geometry of solids with the means provided by plane geometry only. In the case of Yoga if the "depth dimension" be set aside, little remains but an empty husk, of little use not only in the practical but also in the theoretical field; it is little more than an object of curiosity.

Nevertheless, in several Western circles which are serious and not merely interested in vague "spirituality," the possible importance of Yoga in its bearing on the problems besetting the modern mind is beginning to be felt. Significant in this connection is the subtitle given to a collection of studies on Yoga recently published by J. Masui: "The Science of the Whole Man." Another work on the scientific plane recently published is Mircea Eliade's *Yoga: Immortality and Freedom* of which we wish to speak here. Having studied for three years in the University of Calcutta under Surendranath Dasgupta, the wellknown author of several books on Indian philosophy and religion, and having spent some time in the ashram of Rishikesh, near the Himalayas, Eliade would seem to be in an exceptionally favorable position for dealing with this subject. Nevertheless we are inclined to think that Eliade's qualifications for the task he has undertaken are not due to these circumstances, except as regards his mastery of philology, his knowledge of the texts, and his general information. In spite of his undoubted talents, Prof. Dasgupta is a markedly westernized Indian who follows the method of "neutral exposition," and the ashram of Rishikesh, like others more or less accessible, is not so much a center of severe initiation and supervised practice as an environment whose atmosphere is similar to that of the "religious retreats" of the West. Eliade owes his special qualifications to another source; they derive from the fact that before going to India he had acquired knowledge of metaphysical and esoteric doctrines which as such are not of an "official" character. It is essentially to those doctrines that Eliade is indebted for some points of view that place his works on a different plane from those of most writers on oriental ideas and the history of religions. All this, however, is not placed in the foreground. Eliade is very anxious to keep in line with the academic world of the West. Among the many hundreds of authors he quotes it would be difficult to find works that do not enjoy definite academic recognition. One might ask if this does not conceal an attempt to introduce a Trojan Horse into the citadel of official culture, an effort which would seem on the one hand to have met with success, as shown by the favorable and unusually prompt reception given to Eliade's works by those circles, but which is not exempt from the danger of "counter shocks." Our fundamental opinion of Eliade's work on Yoga may be expressed by saying that it is the most complete of all those that have been written on this subject in the domain of the history of religions and of Orientalism. One cannot mention another that for wealth of information, for comparisons, for philological accuracy, for the examination and utilization of all previous contributions, stands on the same level. But when once this has been admitted, some reservations have to be made. In the first place it would seem that the material he handles has often got the better of the writer. I mean to say that in his anxiety to make use of all, really all, that is known on the several varieties of Yoga and on what is directly or indirectly connected therewith, he has neglected the need of discriminating and selecting so as to give importance only to those parts of Yoga that are standard and typical, avoiding the danger that the reader lose track of the essential features by confusing them with the mass of information on secondary matters, variations, and side products. Looking at it from this standpoint, we are even led to wonder whether Eliade's previous book *Yoga, essai sur les origines de la mystique indienne* (Paris, 1936), is not in some respects superior to this last one, which is a reconstruction of the former. In the first book the essential points of reference were more clearly outlined, they were less smothered by the mass of information brought together, and the references to less-known forms of Yoga, such as the Tantric and others, were more clearly pointed out. In the new edition the scrupulous desire to omit nothing has led to the admission of matter which cannot but give a feeling of contamination. Such are the passages on the relations between Yoga and Shamanism and forms of sorcery, necromancy, and even cannibalism present in the religious practices and in the folklore and magic of the natives. Such relationships, even though so studied as to establish the due distances and show the possible "degradations of an ideology due to the incomprehension of the symbolism it contained" may be of interest to the specialist, but they cannot but trouble those who are interested in the superior and "eternal" content of Yoga. Such a reader would have preferred that all such references had been either omitted or abbreviated to the indispensable minimum.

Problems of this kind have, moreover been already dealt with by Eliade in another of his works, *Shamanism: Archaic Techniques of Ecstasy*, and the present references are often nothing but lengthy repetitions. They could have been avoided, thus assuring the new book a character of greater "purity." But for all this, the reader can clearly see here the supreme purpose of the true Yoga, which is the attainment of immortality, the "deconditioning" of the human being, absolute freedom, the active attainment of the "unconditioned." Students of these subjects well know that in Yoga, as in Indian metaphysics in general and still more clearly in Buddhism, immortality has a quite special meaning. In a certain sense, every man is immortal, for according to the doctrine under consideration, death does not end him, but his life is reproduced in an indefinite series of rebirths. The purpose of Yoga is to destroy this immortality, replacing it by that pertaining to a state free from all conditionality, whether cosmic or divine. Eliade calls attention to the fact that existence in the heavens, divine life, what in Western religions is conceived of as Paradise, would seem, judged by this standard, to be a temptation and an arrest: one must place oneself at a point beyond all this. In this connection he might perhaps have quoted the *Sutta* of the "Visit on Brahma" of the *Majjhimonikaya*, where this idea finds its grandest expression. Attention is also called to the part "cognition" plays in the achievement of Yoga, which confers on this achievement a character that might be described as "Olympian." The meaning of cognition as understood by Yoga is indeed that of a "mere awakening producing nothing, which gives immediate revelation of reality," that is to say, of the true nature of the ego, and which thus sets free (p. 42). It is therefore the opposite of a "conquest" understood in the Faustian and atavistic sense, and this should be realized by many modern Western sympathizers with yoga who are following a wrong path. The opposition between the yoga experience and the mystic experience is dearly shown by Eliade. Although he uses the word "mystic" (see also the subtitle of his previous book) in speaking of several matters connected with Yoga, this point is clearly noted by the use he makes of an original expression "enstasy" instead of ecstasy (see pp. 89 ff). "Yoga is not a technique of ecstasy; on the contrary, it endeavors to realize complete concentration, to attain enstasy." As the meaning of "ecstasy" is "out-standing" so the meaning of "enstasy" is "in-standing," a return to the metaphysical center of one's own being as though resuming possession of a throne that has been deserted through that mysterious transcendental fact that Hindu tradition designates by the expression *maya*. While Eliade stresses this opposition particularly in the case of shamanism, it holds good morphologically also for the relations between Yoga and mysticism.

Thus Eliade interprets as "enstasy" *samadhi* itself, the ultimate aim of classical Yoga. And he thus also overcomes the idea of those who, knowing nothing of experiences of this kind, believe that this ultimate term is a kind of trance, a condition of reduced consciousness, almost of unconsciousness ("a zero point between consciousness and unconsciousness" as Rhys Davids said referring to *nirvana*), whereas it is really a state of super-consciousness. The strange thing is that not only Westerners have fallen into so gross an error. We have, for instance, seen D. T. Suzuki suggest an interpretation of this kind (even if in defense of Zen as a specific tendency) in relation to the Yoga of Samkhya and similar mahayanic doctrines. It would perhaps have been useful to develop in this field a comparison between the horizons of Yoga and those of psychoanalysis. All those Westerners who believe they have made such an extraordinary discovery with their psychoanalysis (Jung goes as far as to assert presumptuously, that psychoanalysis alone makes "scientific" understanding of the learning of the East possible) should realize that the positive side of psychoanalysis had been previously discovered centuries and centuries before, by Yoga as part of a full knowledge of man, and not of that mutilated, deformed, and contaminated anthropology, which provides the basis of Freudianism and of all its more or less orthodox derivatives. Reservations must, however, be made as regards that which arouses the Yoga vocation. From the external, historical point of view it is true that Yoga arose from the need of a practical (and we would add: active) experience of sacred things and as a reaction against metaphysical speculations and fossilized ritual. But when it comes to the existentialist motive, we are far from agreeing with Eliade when he writes: "Freedom from suffering, that is *the* principal aim of all Hindu philosophies and all Hindu mysticism" (p. 26). It may appear to be so if only the more popular exoteric aspects of the teaching are taken into account. But this is not true even of Buddhism, as we have shown in one of our works (*The Doctrine of Awakening: The Attainment of Self-Mastery According to the Earliest Buddhist Texts* [London, 1951], pp. 59 ff.); after Stcherbatsky had already shown (*The Central Conception of Buddhism* [London, 1906]) that a deeper meaning could be given to *duhka* than the vulgar one of "pain." The very word *klicta* applied to states of consciousness to be suppressed by the practice of Yoga, properly means "impure" (in a metaphysical, not in a moral sense) and does not mean "painful." The real starting point of Yoga (and of Buddhism itself) is the reaction of a soul aspiring to the absolute as against a contingent, unstable existence, conditioned by agitation, subject to change, existence that includes in its emotional aspects both pain and pleasure and even the beatitude of the most radiant celestial gods. What Eliade states is therefore incorrect, although the book contains matter enough to lead us to a just view of things.

The use in the early chapters of the book of a "vegetative" analogy to describe the Yogic mode of existence, also seems to us unsuitable. Recourse to a "mineral" analogy would be better suited. It would better express Yogic immobility, the "arrest of the flow," the concentration of consciousness on "being" as opposed to "life," and its ritual expressions also: the immobility of the *asana,* the impassiveness of the features, etc. It would perhaps be better, when dealing with the state of existence that has to be overcome, not to introduce the notion of "history," an exclusively Western notion, which finds no match in the world of Hindu metaphysics. In it, as we know, the basic idea is, instead, that of *samsara,* of purely irrational becoming, which differs widely from the notion of "history" and even from the simple condition of temporality for, in the Hindu conception, *samsara* and the world of *maya* are also inclusive of states in which time, as we know it, is non-existent. We have made this remark because Eliade has a special personal notion of his own, which, though it supplies a valuable and legitimate key for the interpretation of many things in the world of myths and rites, is not applicable to all cases. We are dealing with the motive of the destruction of "history" by the return to the prehistoric and a-temporal state of the origins. This scheme can be applied wherever cyclical structures are in evidence. We do not think there is much place for it in the Yoga field. Eliade himself has what is really at issue, i.e., a "break of the level," not only of the level of human, historical experience, whether individual or collective, but also of the cosmic level. The legitimate point of reference is, therefore, that of a doctrine of the multiple states of being, seen as a *vertical system,* whereas the idea of a pre-temporal (prehistoric) origin implies always a residuum of "horizontalism." At a certain point in *samsara* there is an arrest; after which one proceeds not so much backwards as upwards, liberating oneself from all conditioning circumstances. A metaphysical itinerary, this, which in the ancient Western civilization was expressed by the symbolism of the journey through successive planetary spheres and the progressive "unclothing" that took place in each of them while an equivalent of this is given in the Tantric Yoga by the ascent of consciousness transported by the power of the *kundalini* through the seven *chakras*.

We have referred to Tantrism, and one of the principal merits of Eliade's book is that it has dealt fully with this current of Indian spirituality, still little known in the West and which when it has been studied has been generally decried because of its connection with sex magic rites and the use of women. While remaining faithful to the style of "neutral" exposition, more especially in this matter, Eliade suggests the key to interpretations of undoubted value, based always on extensive documentary evidence, as when dealing with the rites of "transubstantiation," "polyvalent languages," etc. So also on the matter of "hyperphysical physiology" or "subtle physiology," which plays an important part in Tantric Yoga, Eliade holds himself afar from the materializing opinions formulated by some Orientalists and some physicians who are ignorant of the very principles underlying such notions. But as Tantric Yoga follows a course which differs widely from that followed by classical Yoga, it would seem likely that important results might have been obtained by engaging in research on typological and morphological lines. It seems to us that in several cases the different forms of Yoga arise not only from technical differences but from a difference in the spirit that inspires them.

The background, which is to some extent immanentistic, of Tantric practices differs substantially from the transcendent one of the Yoga of strict type and of patanjalian orientation. Jnana Yoga and Hatha Yoga (taking the latter in its deeper sense which is not that of "physical Yoga") may have definite differential implications in their general vision of the world (we have referred to it in our work *The Yoga of Power*. We may set up the ideal of liberation against the more positive one of liberty (and here we may refer to the Tantric Siddha and the Kaula whose antinomianism has precedents in some veins of the most ancient Upanishads and Brahmanic literature). The stress laid on the importance of the body in its esoteric aspect may also afford a clue, while it is quite clear that the process of conferring cosmic sense on the body may have a significance of its own which must be referred back to the spirituality of the Vedic origins, and contrasts with the ascetic trends on a dualistic background. These considerations lead us to the much debated problem of the origins of Yoga. It would seem that Eliade is inclined to believe in a non-IndoEuropean, non-"Aryan" origin. In his first book, this view was more stressed and was extended to cover not only Yoga but part of Hindu ascetic tendencies in general. As is known, some inquirers with racial views had already formulated the theory that all forms of asceticism and practices of mortification of the flesh were foreign—*artfremd*—to the spirituality of the Aryan conquerors of India, and that all such notions in Hinduism should be traced back to exogenous influences and to a world-outlook no less foreign—*artfremd*. At first the reference made here was to Dravidian and Kosalian natives; later on the question arose of the archaic civilization brought to light by the excavations at Mohenjo-Daro. It is claimed that among the objects found at Mohenjo-Daro there are figures in the postures— *asana*—of Yogis and ascetics, along with divinities who are not found in the Vedas, while they play an important part in many currents of Yogic and ascetic but also devotional intonation of the later period. All this strikes us as rather problematic for we consider that in such matters morphological considerations must be decisive. Eliade writes: "Yoga, in so far as it represents a reaction against ritualism and scholastic speculation, belongs to the aboriginal tradition and conflicts with the Indo-European [i.e. Aryan] religious heritage" (p. 356). He adds "We should remember that the absence of the Yoga complex in other Indo-European peoples would confirm that this technique is a product of the Asian soil of the Indian territory" (ibid.). All this is not quite right. As regards the first point, we may note that early Buddhism was also a reaction to ritualism and speculation, but it was of purely Aryan origin, starting with the person of its founder. For the rest, the consideration of historical metaphysics must be introduced in a morphological framework that we have already outlined elsewhere (in the already quoted *The Doctrine of Awakening* and also in our *Revolt Against the Modern World*). Account must be taken of that regression of mankind from the spirituality of the origins, to which the traditions of all peoples bear witness and to which, indeed, Eliade himself makes frequent reference in the course of his researches. As a result of this regression, states of spirituality which in the beginning had an almost natural character and were at the basis of a sacramental and ritual conception of the world, were later on attained only exceptionally as the result of ascetic and violent practices. In our opinion this is the historical place of Yoga also, as *spirit*. In other Indo-European traditions it is matched by the Mysteries and initiation practices which, though varying widely in form and method, have the like significance of an experimental *opus restaurationis* and occupy the same position of Yoga when considered in relation to the origins. It may be that in the framework of Hindu spirituality, the transition to a phase of this kind, which corresponds to Yoga, was favored by exogenous influences: *favored*, not *determined.* Beyond possible exterior resemblances of themes, we must consider the possibility that, when passing from one civilization to another, they acquired a widely different meaning. Thus, for instance, it seems pretty certain that the Mohenjo-Daro civilization was essentially a "Mother civilization," a civilization of the "Divine Woman" with a tellurian or lunar background belonging morphologically to the same cycle of southern, paleo-Mediterranean, and even South-American civilizations. The classic spirit of Yoga is, on the other hand, exclusively virile and uranic. We have knowledge of an asceticism which was known also to the Mother civilizations (from the Maya to the Babylonians). But it had a character of mortification which is quite absent from Yoga. Even the central theme of that civilization, the Divine Woman, revives in Hinduism, through the Tantric metaphysics, in a strongly spiritualized form which would be unaccountable if it be not related to the Aryan heritage and to the Upanishads themselves, while its original features survive only in the reemergence of popular orgiastic or devotional cults. The examination of those problems would lead us far afield. But in any case it seems to us that Yoga should be considered only as an integral part of Indo-European spirituality of the purest kind. For this reason also it seems to us that the search for relations with the drosses of Shamanism as they are present in the origins of the Aryan peoples. Or elsewhere, is of no interest. The only thing of interest, as we have said, is the definition of the autonomous features of a spiritual phenomenon which should be examined there where it arose in conformity with its "idea" and therefore in its typical imperfection, liberating itself from empirical conditioning factors.

After this glance at the contents of Eliade's new book we are tempted to inquire of him a somewhat prejudicial question: to whom is the book addressed? As we have openly declared, it is a fundamental work for specialists in the field not only of Oriental research, but also in that of the history of religions. But in his introduction Eliade states that the book is addressed also to a wider public and he speaks of the importance that a knowledge of a doctrine such as that of Yoga may have for the solution of the existential problems of the modern Westerner, confirmed as that doctrine is by immemorial experience. Here complications arise. To meet such a purpose it would be necessary to follow a different plan and to treat the matter in a different way. A Westerner who reads Eliade's book may be able to acquire an idea of Yoga as "*la science intégrale de l'homme* [the integral science of man]," he may acquire knowledge of a teaching that has faced in practice as well as in theory the problem of "deconditioning" man; he will thus add yet one other panorama to the list of the many modern culture has provided him with. His interest will perhaps be more lively than the "neutral" interest of the specialist; he may flirt with the aspects of a "*spiritualite virante.*" But on the existential plane the situation will be pretty much the same as it was before, even if the information available be deeper, more accurate, better documented. The possibility of exercising a more direct influence could only be looked for from a book addressed to those who have shown an interest in Yoga and similar sciences not because they seek for information but because they are seeking for a path; a book that in this special field would remove the misunderstandings, the popular notions, the deviations, and the delusions spread by a certain kind of literature to which we referred at the beginning of this article; a book displaying the accuracy and knowledge that we find in this work of Eliade, in as far as it is an exposition kept within the limits of the history of religions. Such a book has perhaps still to be written. But even so the essential need would not be met, for it is the unanimous opinion of the true masters of Yoga that the key to their science cannot be handed on by the written word.

Fascism: Myth and Reality

Fascism has undergone a process which can be called mythologization, and the attitude which many adopt towards it is of a passionate and irrational kind rather than a critical, intellectual one. This is especially true of those who retain an idealistic loyalty towards the Italy that was. [...] Mythologization has naturally gone hand in hand with idealization, so that only the positive aspects of the Fascist regime are highlighted, deliberately or unconsciously playing down the negative ones. The same procedure is practiced the other way round by those who represent antinationalist forces, their mythologization leading to systematic denigration, the aspects with a view to discrediting it and making everyone hate it. [...] Over and above any polemical one-sidedness, those who, unlike the 'nostalgics' of the younger generation, have lived through Fascism and have thus had a direct experience of the system and its men, know and acknowledge that not everything about it was in order. As long as Fascism existed and could be considered a movement of reconstruction in the making, one of yet unrealized and uncrystalized possibilities, it was still permissible not to criticize it beyond a certain limit. And those who, like ourselves, while defending a set of ideas which only partially coincided with Fascism (and with German National Socialism), did not condemn these movements, even though fully aware of their questionable or aberrant aspects, did so precisely because we counted on future possible developments--to be encouraged with every means and strength we could muster--which might have corrected or eliminated these aspects.

Today, when that Fascism lies behind us as a historical reality, or attitude cannot be the same. Instead of idealizing it in a way consistent with the 'myth' of Fascism, what is necessary now is to separate the positive from the negative, not just for theoretical reasons, but for practical guidance with an eventual political struggle in mind. Thus we should not accept the adjective 'fascist' or 'neo-fascist' tout court; we should call ourselves fascist (if we feel we must) in respect of what was positive about Fascism, not fascist in respect of what Fascism was not. [...] Even in the search for the positive, there is in practice an essential difference between on the one hand those whose only reference point is Fascism (or possible analogous movements of other nations--German National Socialism, Belgian Rexism, the early Falange in Spain, Salazar's Regime, the Romanian Iron Guard: at one point it was possible to talk of a 'world revolution', a general movement of opposition to the proletarian revolution), seeing in it the be-all and end-all of their political, historical, and doctrinal horizons, and on the other those who consider what emerged from such movements as particular manifestations, some more perfect than others, of ideas and principles based in that earlier Tradition of which we have spoken, but adapted to particular circumstances. These principles are to be associated with 'normality' and permanence, relegating what is original and in the strict sense 'revolutionary' about those movements to secondary, contingent traits. In other words, it is a question of making linkages as far as it is possible between the great European political Tradition and discarding what at bottom can be seen as compromises, divergent or even deviant possibilities, or phenomena which were products of the very evils which people set out to take a stand against and fight.

The Nature of Initiatic Knowledge

Those who approach our disciplines must first of all realize this basic point: that the problem and even meaning of knowledge appear in a way very different from the various domains of modern culture. From an initiatic point of view, *to know* does not mean "to think," but *to be* the known object. Something is not really known until it is *realized*, or, in other words, until one's consciousness is transformed into it. In these terms, knowledge is one and the same with *experience* ; thus, the initiatic method is a purely experimental method. As far as certainty is concerned, what counts here is what one has learned through direct and individual experience. In ordinary life, every sensation, every yearning, emotion, or direct perception (a pain, a desire, an intuition) has this character. To speak here of "true" and "false" is meaningless; what matters is the knowledge of the thing itself according to an absolute "Is," or to an experienced "Is" that does not wait for intellectual recognition. In this type of knowledge, there are no degrees or approximations or probabilities; one either has it or hasn't it. However, for the ordinary man such knowledge is restricted to the sensible order, which has a finite, contingent, and accidental character. That which he ordinarily regards as knowledge is something different; it is a system of concepts, relations, and hypotheses that no longer has a pragmatic but rather an abstract character. The immediate data of experience, namely that which is directly evident to one's consciousness, are usually regarded as mere "phenomena"; one tends to posit or assume the existence *behind* them of something to which one attributes the character of true and objective reality. For science, this "something" is matter, or the varied interplay of etheric vibrations; for the philosophers, it is the "noumenon" or the "thing in itself" or some other vague idea of theirs; for religion, it is some sort of divine hypostasis. Generally speaking, this is the situation: a body of knowledge is organized--- profane knowledge --- that does not go beyond purely sensible experience and which has a certain degree of objectivity only through transcending everything that has the value of individual and living evidence, vision, and meaning realized by consciousness. What emerges is an antithesis: what is pure experience, due to its finite and phenomenal character, is not "knowledge," just as that which is regarded as "knowledge" is not experience.

The initiatic path goes beyond this antithesis, pointing to an essentially different direction in which the criterion of direct experience is never abandoned. While for ordinary people this experience is one and the same with sensible experience, the initiatic teaching claims the possibility of many forms of experience, of which the former is just one. Each of these forms corresponds to a given way of perceiving reality; they are susceptible to being transformed into one another and to arrange themselves in a hierarchical fashion, in levels of perception that have an increasingly higher degree of absoluteness. According to such perspectives, there is no "world of phenomena" and an "absolute" behind them; what is "phenomenal" is merely that which characterizes a certain degree of experience and a certain state of the Self, while what is "absolute" is that which is correlative to another degree of experience and to another state of the Self, which the former may generate through an appropriate transformation.

As far as the measure of absoluteness is concerned, one may say approximately that it is determined by the degree of *active identification*, namely by the degree according to which the Self is implicated and unified in its experience, and according to which it object is transparent to it in terms of a *meaning*. In correspondence to these degrees, the hierarchy proceeds from "sign" to "sign," from "name" to "name," until it reaches a state of perfect, super-rational, intellectual vision, of full actualization or realization of the object of the Self and the Self in the object. That is a state both of power and of absolute evidence in regard to what is known; once this state is reached, every rationalization and speculation appears superfluous and every discussion meaningless. There is an ancient saying according to which one did not join the ancient Mysteries in order "to learn," but rather in order to achieve a sacred state through a deep experience.

As a consequence of this, the initiatic teaching considers more negatively than positively the tendency of the mind to wander in the interpretation and solution of this or that philosophical problem, to erect theories and to be interested in some or another view of profane science. All this is useless and leads nowhere. The real problem has only a *practical* and operative character. What are the means to obtain the transformation and integration of my experience? This is what one should be concerned about. This is why initiation in the West has been associated less with the concept of a cognitive process than with that of an Art (*Ars Regia*) or of a Work (*opus magnum*, or *opus magicum*), or of a symbolic construction (the construction of the "Temple"), while in China the notions of the Absolute and of a *way* converge in one term, "Tao." It is therefore evident that the more or less Theosophical spiritualism that today fills the heads of its devotees with all kinds of speculations and fantasies about cosmology and supersensible worlds and beings can only foster an attitude that is flawed from the start. Only the experiential and practical attitude of a restrained mind and a silent and secret action performed under the aegis of the golden Hermetic saying "post laborem scientia" (knowledge after work) is healthy and valid from an initiatic point of view. I dare say that this applies to everything else for which modern "educated" men claim superiority and the right to hold opinions on. Culture in the modern, profane sense does not constitute a necessary presupposition, nor a privileged condition for spiritual realization. Quite the contrary: a person who has remained outside the crossroads of culture, "psychology," and the various aesthetic and literary contaminations, but who display an open mind, balance, and courage is more qualified to receive a superior knowledge than any academic professor, writer, or "critical thinker" of our day and age. Therefore, those who *really* amount to something in the initiatic order can be recognized by their extreme reluctance to theorize and argue. If these people discern a sincere aspiration in you, they will tell you only this: "There is the problem, and the these are the means: go ahead." Another consequence of the initiatic concept of knowledge is the principle of *differentiation* , which is also in distinct contrast with the ideas that inform modern profane knowledge. In fact, the entire modern "culture" (with science at the forefront) is dominated by a democratic, leveling, and uniform tendency. This culture regards as an "acquisition" what is within everyone's reach: thus, according to modern culture, a truth is such only when everyone can recognize it, provided they have reached a certain level of education or, at most, pursued some studies, which nevertheless leave them the same as they always were. This may be true in the case of something conceptual and abstract, to be put in someone's head like something into a sack. But when it comes to experience, and more specifically to an experience conditioned by an essential transformation of the substance of consciousness, precise limits must arise. The knowledge acquired in this way cannot possibly be within everyone's reach, nor can it be transmitted to everyone without thereby degrading and desecrating it. There are different sorts of knowledge, and their differentiation corresponds to that which initiation, in its various degrees, brings about in human nature. This knowledge cannot be truly understood or "realized" by any but those who are at the same level, or who have an equal degree in a hierarchy that is endowed with a rigorously objective and ontological character. Thus, even aside from those occult or Theosophical expositions that are mere divagations or fantasies, in regard to initiatic and effective esoteric knowledge, the uselessness of merely theoretical communication and propagation is again confirmed. To reduce initiatic knowledge to a "theory" is the worst thing one can do. Here more than ever it is *allusion* and *symbol* that serve to produce illuminations. But if, as a result, there is no *beginning of an inner movement*, even this has no value. The very character of initiatic knowledge demands differentiation. It is natural that those who regard ordinary existence and sensible experience as the beginning and end of everything lack any common ground with that which, in its essence, is *realization*. All this should be seen with perfect clarity, and also its natural consequence: either to give up or to recognize different criteria of truth and knowledge from those predominant in modern culture and thought. The way of initiation is one that establishes substantial differences among human beings and reaffirms the principle of *suum cuique* (to each his own) against the egalitarian and uniform view of knowledge: according to this principle, one's knowledge, truth, and freedom are proportional to what one is. One objection worth addressing may come from someone used to operating among tangible things and "concrete" ideas, who may say that transcendent states of being and the experiences mentioned (even if they can be achieved, since they are enclosed in the "subjective" sphere) merely amount to mysticism: that the criterion of knowledge as experience and identification is more or less one of mere feeling, and therefore it does not produce any insight when explaining, understanding, or giving an account of external things and of what takes place in us. These objections will be analyzed in greater depth further on. At this point, it is enough to clarify two points. First, when we talk initiatically about "identification," what we mean is always an *active* identification, not a confusing and merging with or sinking into something: it is not an infra-intellectual and emotive state, but a state of essential and super-rational clarity. Here lies the difference between the mystical and the initiatic spheres; it is an essential difference, even though not immediately evident to those who, apart from things and abstract concepts, can see only a dark night in which, for them, all cats are black.

The second point concerns the very notion of "explaining," although if we pursued this issue, it would lead us too far. We should begin by turning the tables against the objection and asserting that none of the profane disciplines has ever, nor ever will, provide any *real explanation* whatsoever. Those who, in order to "explain," attempt to show that the contrary is inconceivable, must indicate how they can really "explain" something outside the abstract domain of mathematics and formal logic (in which "rational necessity" or the inconceivability of the contrary is reduced to mere coherence in regard to the propositions previously agreed upon). We intend to refer to concrete reality. However, here, from a rational point of view, there is absolutely nothing that exists simply because its opposite is inconceivable *a priori*. There is nothing in regard to which, beside various pseudo-explanations, one could not ask: "Why thus and not otherwise?" Ancient and traditional science, to which initiatic knowledge is related, has followed an essentially different path, namely the path of knowledge of the effects in their real causes, of the "facts" in the powers of which they are the manifestations, which is the equivalent of the *identification with the causes* in the terms of a "magical" state. Only such a state can lead to the absolute rationale of a phenomenon; only this state can "explain" it in an eminent sense, because in it that phenomenon is grasped, or even *seen*, in its real genesis.

The important consequence of this is that on the initiatic path the acquisition of knowledge parallels the acquisition of power, since the active identification with a cause of virtually confers a power over that same cause. Modern men believe that this is the same in the case of their science, since through various techniques science brings about well-known material realizations; and yet they grossly mistaken, since the power afforded by technology is no more a true power than the explanations of profane sciences are true explanations. The cause , in both cases, is the same; it is the fact of a man who remains a man, and who does not change his nature to any significant degree. This is why the possibilities afforded by technology have a "democratic" and even *immoral* character, like its corresponding knowledge: differences between individuals mean nothing to them. It is a power consisting of automatism, which belongs to everyone and to no one; a power that is not a *value* , nor *justice* , which can make a person powerful without making him superior at the same time.

However, this is possible only because, in the world of technology, one does not and cannot speak of a true *act* , namely an action that begins directly from the Self and affirms itself in the order of real causes. Being absolutely mechanical and inorganic, hence lacking relations with the essence of the Self, the world of technology represents the antithesis of anything that may have the character of real power, created out of superiority, or stamped with superiority, incommunicable, inalienable, spiritual. We must acknowlege that many man today, for all his knowledge of phenomena and through surrounded by his countless diabolical machines, is as miserable and lost as ever; spiritually, he is a worse barbarian than those whom he presumed to call by this name; he is increasingly conditioned rather than conditioning, and thus he is exposed to reactions in an interplay of irrational forces that ephemeralize the mirage of his exclusively material power and things. He is farther away from the path of self-realization than man was in any other civilization, because a surrogate of knowledge and power that one may well call diabolical replaces authentic knowledge and power in him.

In the initiatic domain, we repeat, authentic knowledge is justice, sanction of a dignity, natural and inalienable, emanation of an integrated life, according to the well-defined degrees of such an integration. Just as in this order of things knowledge achieved beyond the uncertainty and ambiguity of sensible phenomena does not refer to formulae or to abstract explicative principles, but rather to real beings grasped through immediate spiritual perception----likewise, the ideal of power here is that of an action occurring not subject to natural laws, but above them; not among phenomena, but among the causes of phenomena, with the irresistibility and the right proper to him who is superior. And this superiority comes from having effectively disengaged himself from the human condition, and from having achieved the initiatic awakening.

The Different Meanings of Race

The racialist consideration of man cannot stop at a mere biological level, otherwise it would be worthy of the accusation by the Jew Trotsky of it being just "zoological materialism." It is also not enough to say, like Walter Gross, that "in the concept of race we intend that completeness of human life, in which body and spirit, matter and soul, are fused in a superior unity," and that deciding whether one of the two things is determined by the other. Whether bodily form is determined by the soul or vice-versa is an extra scientific, metaphysical problem which is not a consideration of racialism. Even less satisfactory is the following statement by Alfred Rosenberg: "We do not agree with the proposition that the spirit creates the body, nor with the inverse, that the body creates the spirit. There is no clear boundary between the spiritual world and the physical world: both constitute an indivisible whole."

If race is no longer to be considered a myth, but as the object of a doctrine, then one cannot stop at these levels.

The concept of race assumes different meanings not only as applied man and to animal species, but also regarding different human types. We therefore must lay a primary distinction: that which lies between the "races of nature" and those of a higher, more human and spiritual, sense.

From a methodological point of view, it is absurd to consider racialism as a self-contained discipline instead of being strictly dependent on a general theory of man. The manner in which the human being is conceived affects the essence of any doctrine of race. If it is conceived in a materialistic manner, this materialism will display itself in the corresponding concept of race; if it is a spiritualistic manner, then the racial concept will also be so. Even when considering that which is material in the human and depends on the laws of matter, the racial doctrine should never forget the hierarchical place and the functional dependence possessed by matter in the whole of the human being.

Man distinguishes himself from the animal by his participation in a supernatural, superbiological element, and only by this participation can he be free or be himself.

The distinction in the human being of the three different principles of body, soul, and spirit is fundamental to the traditional vision of man. In a more or less complete form, one finds this distinction in all ancient traditions, and it was continued during the Middle Ages; the Aristotelian-Scholastic conception of the three souls," vegetative, sensitive and intellectual; the trinity of soma, psyche and nous; the Roman one of corpus, mens and anima; the Indo-Aryan trinity of sthula-, linga- and karana-sarira, are as many equivalent expressions of that distinction. It is furthermore important to emphasize that this view is not to be considered as a particular "philosophical" interpretation amongst many others, but as objective, and impersonal knowledge which adheres to the very same nature of things.

As a basic explanation of the three concepts, it can be said that the spirit, in the traditional conception, has always meant something supernatural and superindividual; it has therefore nothing to do with the common intellect and less still with the pale world of "thinkers" and "men of letters." It is instead the element which focuses the basis of any virile ascent, heroic elevation, or effort to achieve in life what is "more than life."

In classic antiquity, the spirit, as nous or anima, was opposed to the soul as the masculine principle is opposed to the feminine, or as the solar element is opposed to the lunar. The soul already belongs to the world of becoming more than that of being; it is connected to the vital powers, as well as to all perceptive faculties and to any passions. With its unconscious ramifications, it establishes the connection between spirit and body. From this view, one must acknowledge that the inequality of mankind is not only physical, biological or anthropological, but also psychic and spiritual. Men are not only different in body, but also in soul and spirit.

According to this, the racial doctrine must articulate itself in three degrees.

Races of Nature and Superior Races

Man, instead of letting the center of himself fall where it is normal, e.g., in the spirit, can let it fall in one of the subordinate elements, in the psychic element or the physical element, which will then take over as the directive part and reduce the superior elements to the role of instruments. By extending this view, from the single to those larger individualities called races, one reaches the above-mentioned distinction between races of nature and the truly human races.

Some races can be compared to the man or animal who, degrading himself, has arrived at a purely animalistic way of life: such are the races of nature. They are not enlightened by any superior element, by any force from above in which their life in space and time takes place.

Because of this, the collectivistic elements predominate in them, as instinct, as characteristic of the species, as the spirit and unity of the horde.

In other races, the naturalistic element preserves its normal function of vehicle and expressive tool of a superior, superbiological element which is to the first as the spirit is to the body in an individual.

In these races, behind a race of the body, of the blood and of the soul, there lies a race of the spirit. Such a truth was distinctly felt wherever the history attributed "divine" or "celestial" origins to a given race, stock or caste, and supernatural, "heroic" traits to the leader or to its primeval legislator.

Racialism of the Second Degree – the Race of the Soul

As racialism of the second degree, one means a theory of the race of the soul and a typology of the soul of the race. Such racialism has to recognize the primary and irreducible elements which act from the inside, so that groups of individuals manifest a constant way of being or "style" in their actions, thoughts, and feelings.

Here we come to a new concept of racial purity of a given type: it is no longer a question, like in the race of the first degree (based on purely biological considerations), to ascertain whether a given individual presents that given group of physical characteristics; it is a question of establishing whether the race of the body borne by a given individual is the adequate, conforming expression of his race of the soul, and vice-versa. If this is the case, the type is pure from the second degree point of view.

We can consider the Rassenseelekunde or "psychoanthropology" of L. F. Clauss as being racialism of the second degree. He emphasized the necessity of such research with convincing examples. Let us consider, for example, the phenomenon of mutual understanding. In everyday life there are many cases of persons who are of the same physical race, stock, or sometimes even – as in the case of brothers or fathers and sons – the same line, who do not succeed in understanding one another. A boundary separates their souls and their way of feeling and seeing is different. A common race of body or line is not enough to bridge such differences. The possibility of understanding, and thus of true solidarity, can only exist where there is a common race of the soul.

Racialism of the Third Degree – the Race of the Spirit

Racial research of the third degree, as we know, concerns the races of the spirit. It is truly the research that pursues the concept of races to its ultimate root, wherever it is a question of normal civilizations and superior human stocks; a root which communicates with superpersonal, super-ethical and metaphysical forces.

For such research, the specific manner of conceiving both the sacred and the supernatural, as well as the relationship of man with himself, the vision of life in the highest sense, and the entire world of symbols and myths, all this constitutes a very positive and objective subject, just as facial traits and cranial structures constitute positive determinations for the race of the first degree.

In the field of the third degree racial doctrine, the signs of "vertical," superhistorical heredity are of the utmost importance.

As a first step it is necessary to eliminate the evolutionist myth in all its forms, since it is evident that, if one continues to believe that the more one goes back in time, the more one sinks into to the horror of bestial barbarity, then it would be madness to pretend to obtain points of reference valid for the present from prehistoric investigation.

Wherever there exists any evolutionist premise, the research of the origins and the emphasis on the principle of heredity would fatally lead to such aberrations as those contained in certain psychoanalytical exegeses like the "totem and taboo" of Freud.

Our official culture, which calls itself "serious" and "critical" and which is lamentable and largely represented in our schools, insists on considering myth as either an arbitrary creation of the "pre-philosophical" conscience, or as something pertaining to forms of inferior religions, or as superstitious interpretations of mere natural phenomena, or finally as part of "folklore"; without mentioning the "discoveries" of psychoanalysis and of the so-called "sociological school," both typical creations of Judaism.

We must return to conceiving myth and symbol as they were conceived by the ancient, traditional man, e.g., as the expression peculiar to a super-rational reality, almost as the seal of those metaphysical forces which acted within the depth of the races, traditions, religions and the historic and prehistoric civilizations.

The Occult War

Various causes have been adduced to explain the crisis that has affected and still affects the life of modern peoples: historical, social, socioeconomic, political, moral, and cultural causes, according to different perspectives. The part played by each of these causes should not be denied. However, we need to ask a higher and essential question: are these always the first causes and do they have an inevitable character like those causes found in the material world? Do they supply an ultimate explanation or, in some cases, is it necessary to identify influences of a higher order, which may cause what has occurred in the West to appear very suspicious, and which, beyond the multiplicity of individual aspects, suggest that there is the same logic at work? The concept of occult war must be defined within the context of the dilemma. The occult war is a battle that is waged imperceptibly by the forces of global subversion, with means and in circumstances ignored by current historiography.

The notion of occult war belongs to a three dimensional view of history: this view does not regard as essential the two superficial dimensions of time and space (which include causes, facts, and visible leaders) but rather emphasizes the dimension of depth, or the "subterranean" dimension in which forces and influences often act in a decisive manner, and which, more often not than not, cannot be reduced to what is merely human, whether at an individual or a collective level.

Having said that, it is necessary to specify the meaning of the term "subterranean." We should not think, in this regard, of a dark and irrational background which stands in relation to the known forces of history as the unconscious stands to consciousness, in the way the latter relationship is discussed in the recently developed "Depth Psychology." If anything, we can talk about the unconscious only in regard to those who, according to the three-dimensional view, appear to be history's objects rather than its subjects, since in their thoughts and conduct they are scarcely aware of the influences which they obey and the goals that they contribute toward achieving. In these people, the center falls more in the unconscious and the pre-conscious than in the clear reflected consciousness, no matter what they–who are often men of action and ideologues–believe. Considering this relation, we can say that the most decisive actions of the occult war take place in the human unconscious. However, if we consider the true agents of history in the special aspects we are now discussing, things are otherwise: here we cannot talk of the subconscious or the unconscious, since we are dealing with intelligent forces that know very well what they want and what are the means most suited to achieve their objectives. The third dimension of history should not be diluted in the fog of abstract philosophical or sociological concepts, but should rather be thought of as a "backstage" dimension where specific "intelligences" are at work.

An investigation of the secret history that aspires to be positivist and scientific should not be too lofty or removed from reality. However, it is necessary to assume as the ultimate reference point a dualistic scheme not dissimilar from the one found in an older tradition. Catholic historiography used to regard history not only as a mechanism of natural, political, economic, and social causes, but also as the unfolding of divine Providence, to which hostile forces are opposed. These forces are sometimes referred to in a moralistic fashion as "forces of evil," or in a theological fashion as the "forces of the Anti-Christ." Such a view has a positive content, provided it is purified and emphasized by bringing it to a less religious and more metaphysical plane, as was done in Classical and Indo-European antiquity: forces of the cosmos against forces of chaos.

To the former correspond everything that is form, order, law, spiritual hierarchy, and tradition in the higher sense of the word; to the latter correspond every influence that disintegrates, subverts, degrades, and promotes the predominance of the inferior over the superior, matter over spirit, quantity over quality. This is what can be said in regard to the ultimate reference points of the various influences that act upon the realm of tangible causes, behind known history. These must be taken into account, though with some prudence. Let me repeat: aside from this necessary metaphysical background, let us never lose sight of concrete history.

Methodologically speaking, we need to be careful to prevent valid insights from degenerating into fantasies and superstition, and not develop the tendency to see an occult background everywhere and at all costs. In this regard, every assumption we make must have the character of what are called "working hypotheses" in scientific research: as when something is admitted provisionally, thus allowing the gathering and arranging of a group of apparently isolated facts, only to confer on them a character not of hypothesis but of truth when, at the end of a serious inductive work, the data converge in validating the original assumption. Every time an effect outlasts and transcends its tangible causes, a suspicion should arise, and a positive or negative influence behind the stages should be perceived. A problem is posited, but in analyzing it and seeking its solution, prudence must be exercised. The fact that those who have ventured in this direction have not restrained their wild imaginations has discredited what could have been a science, the results of which could hardly be overestimated. This too meets the expectations of the hidden enemy.

After considering the state of society and modern civilization, one should ask if this is not a specific case that requires the application of this method; in other words, one should ask whether some situations of real crisis and radical subversion in the modern world can be satisfactorily explained through "natural" and spontaneous processes, or whether we need to refer to something that has been concerted, namely a still unfolding plan, devised by forces hiding in the shadows.

bibliography

- *Tao Tê Ching: Il libro della via e della virtù* (1923; *The Book of the Way and Virtue*). Second edition:*Il libro del principio e della sua azione*(1959;*The Book of the Primary Principle and of Its Action*).

- *Saggi sull'idealismo magico* (1925;*Essays on Magical Idealism*).

- *L'individuo e il divenire del mondo*(1926;*The Individual and the Becoming of the World*).

- *L'uomo come potenza*(1927;*Man as Potency*).

- *Teoria dell'individuo assoluto*(1927;*The Theory of the Absolute Individual*).

- *Imperialismo pagano* (1928; second edition 1932); English translation: *Pagan Imperialism.* Gornahoor Press. 2017.

- *Introduzione alla magia* (1927–1929; 1971); English translation: *Introduction to Magic: Rituals and Practical Techniques for the Magus.* Inner Traditions/Bear. 2001.

- *Fenomenologia dell'individuo assoluto*(1930;*The Phenomenology of the Absolute Individual*).

- *La tradizione ermetica*(1931); English translation: *The Hermetic Tradition: Symbols and Teachings of the Royal Art.* Inner Traditions/Bear. 1995.

- *Maschera e volto dello spiritualismo contemporaneo: Analisi critica delle principali correnti moderne verso il sovrasensibile*(1932); English translation:*The Mask and Face of Contemporary Spiritualism.* Arktos. 2018.

- *Rivolta contro il mondo moderno* (1934; second edition 1951; third edition 1970); English translation:*Revolt Against the Modern World: Politics, Religion, and Social Order in the Kali Yuga.* Inner Traditions/Bear. 1995.

- *Tre aspetti del problema ebraico* (1936; English translation: *Three Aspects of the Jewish Problem,* Thompkins & Cariou 2003.

- *Il Mistero del Graal e la Tradizione Ghibellina dell'Impero*(1937); English translation:*The Mystery of the Grail: Initiation and Magic in the Quest for the Spirit*. Inner Traditions/Bear. 1996.

- *Il mito del sangue. Genesi del Razzismo*(1937; second edition 1942); English translation:*The Myth of the Blood: The Genesis of Racialism*. Arktos. 2018.

- *Indirizzi per una educazione razziale* (1941; (*The Elements of Racial Education*).

- *Sintesi di dottrina della razza* (1941). (*Synthesis of a Doctrine of Race*)

- *La dottrina del risveglio*(1943); English translations:*The Doctrine of Awakening: The Attainment of Self-Mastery According to the Earliest Buddhist Texts*. Inner Traditions/Bear. 1996.

- *Lo Yoga della potenza* (1949); English translation: *The Yoga of Power: Tantra, Shakti, and the Secret Way*. Inner Traditions/Bear. 1993.

- *Orientamenti, undici punti* (1950); English translation:*"Orientations: Eleven Points", in A Traditionalist Confronts Fascism*. Arktos. 2015.

- *Gli uomini e le rovine* (1953); English translation: *Men Among the Ruins: Post-War Reflections of a Radical Traditionalist*. Inner Traditions/Bear. 2002.

- *Metafisica del sesso* (1958); English translations: 1983 – 1991: *Eros and the Mysteries of Love: The Metaphysics of Sex*. Inner Traditions/Bear. 1991.

- *Cavalcare la tigre*(1961); English translation: *Ride the Tiger: A Survival Manual for the Aristocrats of the Soul*. Inner Traditions/Bear. 2003.

- *Il cammino del cinabro* (1963; second edition 1970); English translation: *The Path of Cinnabar*. Arktos. 2009.

- *L'arco e la clava*(1968); English translation: *The Bow and the Club*. Arktos. 2018.

- *Meditazioni delle vette*(1974); English translation: **Meditations on the Peaks: Mountain Climbing as Metaphor for the Spiritual Quest.** Inner Traditions/Bear. 1998.

- *Il fascismo visto valla destra; Note sul terzo Reich* (1974) ; English translation: **Fascism Viewed from the Right.** Arktos. 2013..And:**Notes on the Third Reich.** Arktos. 2013.

- *Ricognizioni. Uomini e problemi*(1974); English translation:**Recognitions: Studies on Men and Problems from the Perspective of the Right.** Arktos. 2017.

- *Metafisica della Guerra*(1996); English translation:**Metaphysics of War: Battle, Victory and Death in the World of Tradition.** Arktos. 2011.

Made in the USA
Middletown, DE
04 May 2021